MUSEOPATHY

Diane Borsato
John Dickson
Fastwürms
Jamelie Hassan
Peter Hobbs
Barb Hunt
Brian Jungen
Komar & Melamid
with William McClelland
Linda Montano
Anne Ramsden
Clive Robertson
Mitch Robertson
Joyce Wieland
Mel Ziegler

This publication documents the exhibition MUSEOPATHY, organized by the Agnes Etherington Art Centre, and the performance event EMPATHOLOGY, produced by DisplayCult, presented at Kingston heritage sites and museums 23 June to 9 September 2001.

Curated by Jim Drobnick and Jennifer Fisher

ISBN 0-88911-908-2

EDITOR: Jan Allen

COPY EDITOR: Steve Anderson

DESIGN: Associés libres, Montréal

PRE-PRESS: Photosynthèse

PRINTERS: Litho Acme-Renaissance

PHOTOGRAPHERS: Dean Baldwin p. 60-61, 64, 66, 67 (right), 68 (above), 70, 71, 74-75, 77-78; Spencer Bardell p. 24, 25, 31 (above), 33 (below), 49 (below), 90; Jerry Browne p. 34-35; John Dickson p. 20, 23 (above); Jim Drobnick p. 26, 31 (left), 33, 38 (left), 39, 52, 59 (above), 73; Fastwürms p. 27; Julie Fiala p. 51 (below); Jennifer Fisher p. 31 (right), 49 (above); Nikki Forrest p. 67 (left), 72, 79 (right); York Lethbridge p. 22, 23 (below), 28 (above), 31 (second from right), 36, 41, 50 (left), 57; Paul Litherland p. 6, 12, 31 (second from left), 38 (right), 58, 59 (below), 80, 83, 86-87, 88, 92-93, 94, 95, 98, 99-104; Anne Ramsden p. 44, 46, 47; Clive Robertson p. 79 (1-3 left)

COVER IMAGE: Fastwürms, detail, *Ms. Rockhound 2001*. Photo: York Lethbridge

PUBLISHER: Agnes Etherington Art Centre, Queen's University, in association with DisplayCult

DISTRIBUTION: ABC Art Books Canada, www.ABCartbookscanada.com

Thanks to contributors and special supporters:

Douglas Arnberg, www.sub-aquatic.com
Candice Christmas, Kingston Economic Development Corporation
Concordia University Part-Time Faculty Association
Inter-Arts Program of the Canada Council for the Arts
Barbara Fischer, Blackwood Gallery, Erindale College, University of Toronto
Ken McGuirk and the Parks Department of the City of Kingston
Jocelyn Purdie
Kingston Guitar Shop
Information Technology Systems, Queen's University
Summer Work Experience Program, Queen's University
Irving A. Rosen, KIMCO Steel Sales Ltd.
Robert A. Wood, 8020 Info Inc.
Young Canada Works Program, Department of Heritage

Agnes Etherington Art Centre, Queen's University
Kingston, Ontario, Canada K7L 3N6 www.queensu.ca/ageth

DISPLAYCULT www.displaycult.com

ONTARIO ARTS COUNCIL
CONSEIL DES ARTS DE L'ONTARIO

THE COMMUNITY FOUNDATION OF GREATER KINGSTON

KINGSTON CANADA

Ontario Cultural Attractions Fund OCAF FACO

THE KINGSTON WHIG-STANDARD

Canada Council for the Arts Conseil des Arts du Canada

MUSEOPATHY

curated by
Jim Drobnick and Jennifer Fisher

Agnes Etherington Art Centre, Queen's University
in association with *DisplayCult*

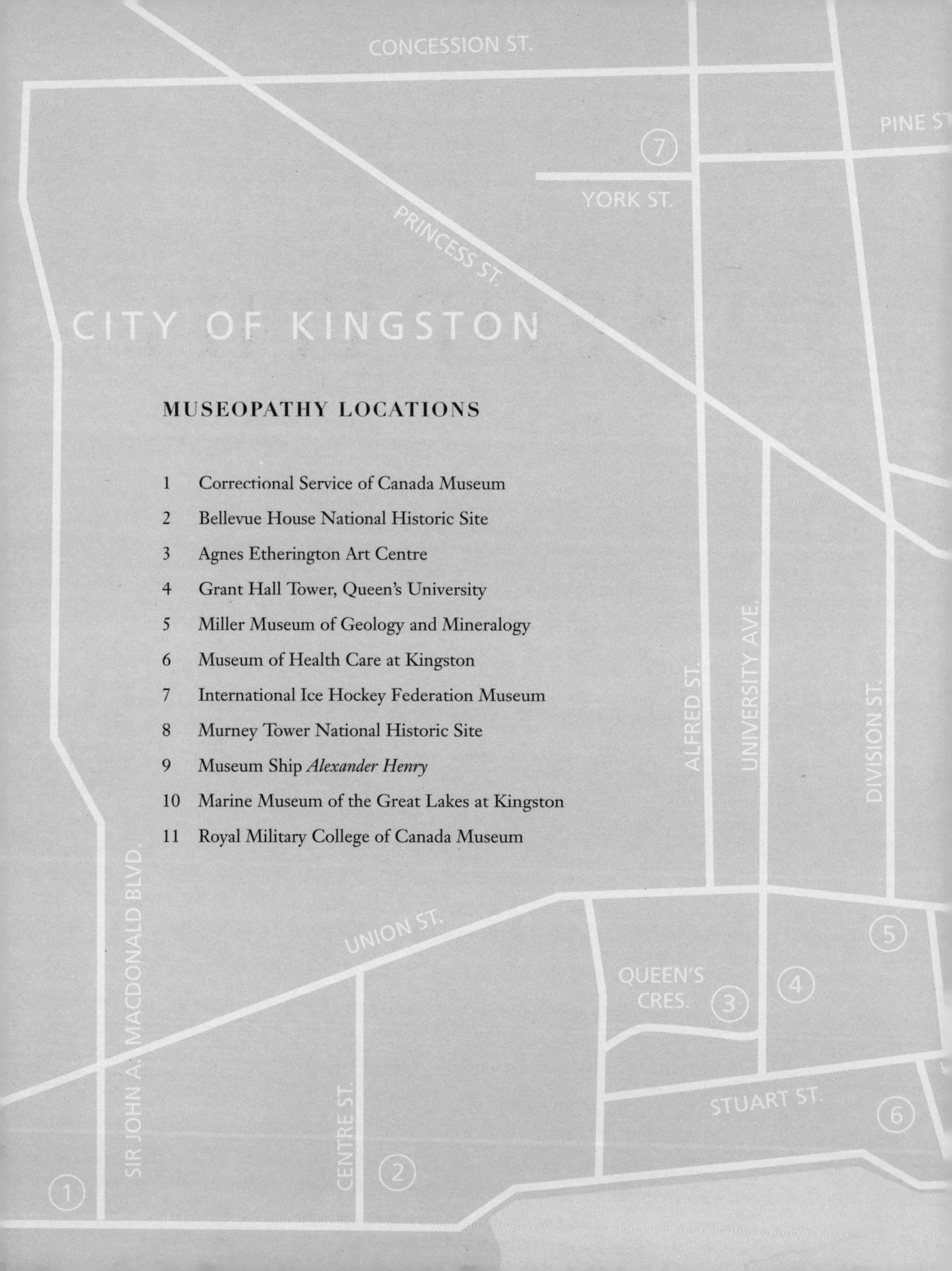

MUSEOPATHY LOCATIONS

1 Correctional Service of Canada Museum
2 Bellevue House National Historic Site
3 Agnes Etherington Art Centre
4 Grant Hall Tower, Queen's University
5 Miller Museum of Geology and Mineralogy
6 Museum of Health Care at Kingston
7 International Ice Hockey Federation Museum
8 Murney Tower National Historic Site
9 Museum Ship *Alexander Henry*
10 Marine Museum of the Great Lakes at Kingston
11 Royal Military College of Canada Museum

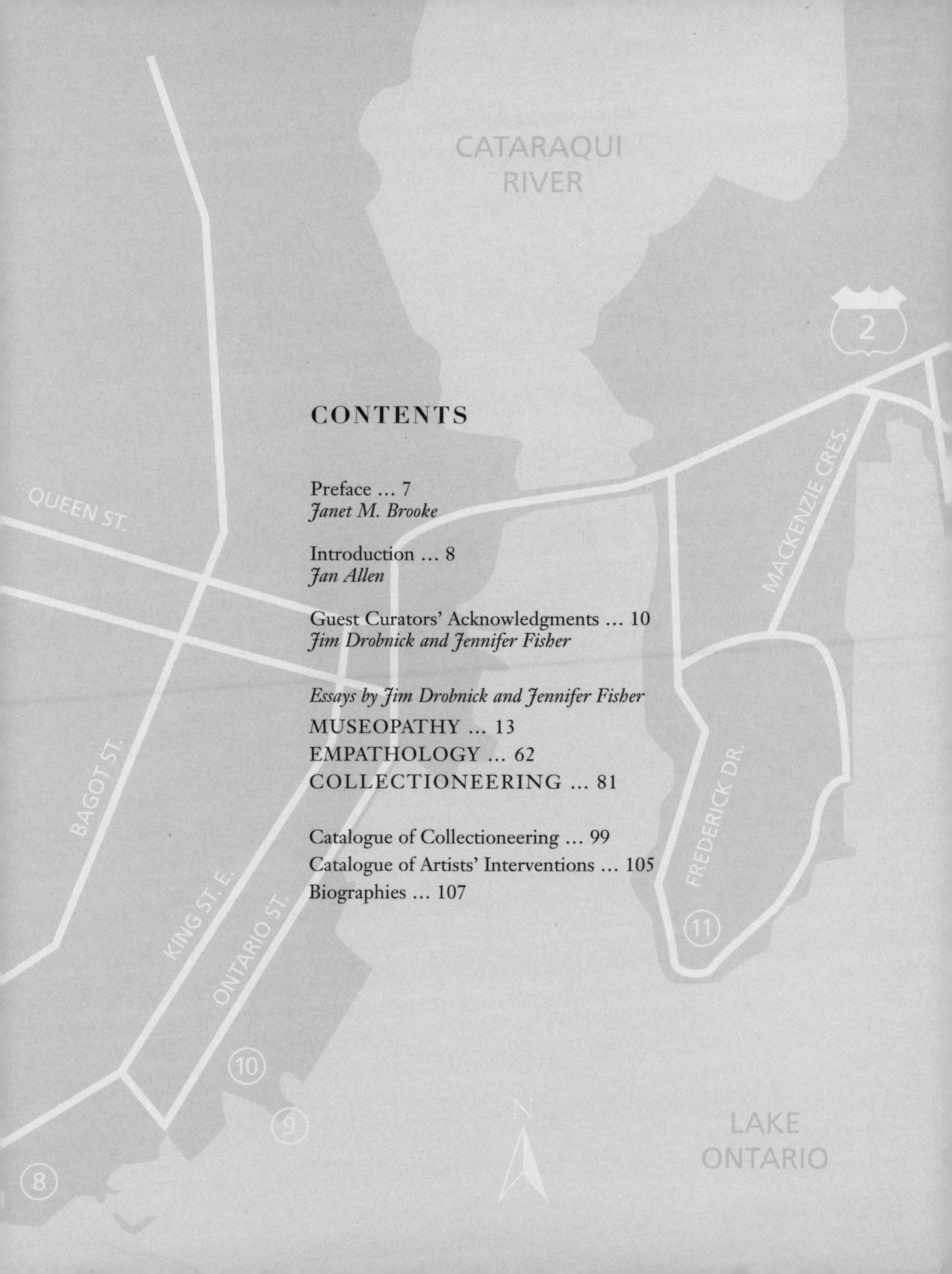
CATARAQUI
RIVER
QUEEN ST.
BAGOT ST.
KING ST. E.
ONTARIO ST.
MACKENZIE CRES.
FREDERICK DR.
2
8
9
10
11
N
LAKE
ONTARIO

CONTENTS

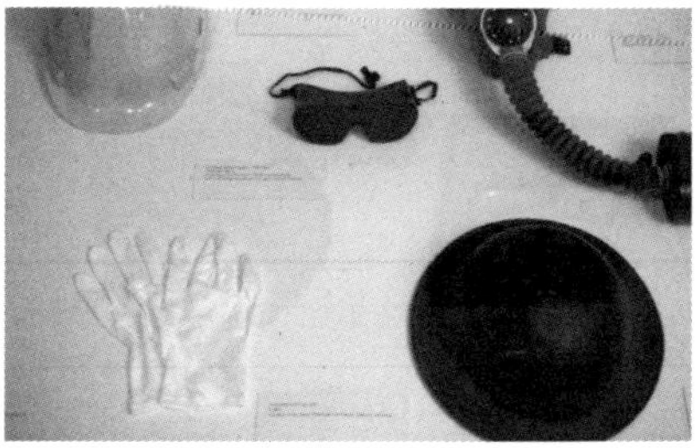

Collectioneering: Constellation #4

PREFACE

ONE MIGHT EASILY BE ACCUSED OF PIRACY in appending one's text to a body of work in which one played no part, yet as the recent incoming director of the Agnes Etherington Art Centre, I would be equally remiss in seeing this fine publication go to press without comment. MUSEOPATHY — as an exhibition and through this post-event record — has been an extraordinary experience for the Art Centre and for Kingston, not only for the breadth and originality of its reach, but also for its incisiveness and pertinence to issues of culture and community.

Through MUSEOPATHY, organizing curator Jan Allen and guest curators Jim Drobnick and Jennifer Fisher challenge us to consider contemporary art practice, and the role of the art gallery as its privileged and exclusive venue, in new ways — new ways that have strong historical antecedents. Drawing on Renaissance and Baroque notions of the *wunderkammer* (a.k.a. cabinet of curiosities), MUSEOPATHY's curatorial concept apposed works of art with objects and artifacts into a postmodern iteration of that most traditional European concept which held that "wonders of God," "wonders of nature" and "wonders of man" could co-exist seamlessly, in ways that defy norms of logic and classification so cherished in Western culture since the Age of Enlightenment. In so doing, the exhibition confronted the very idea of the modern gallery, where such preoccupations are deeply rooted. Similarly, by siting commissioned works of art and performances in museums and heritage sites throughout the city, it reaffirmed the role of art practice outside conventional gallery boundaries. Such reciprocities — works of art inserted into non-gallery space, and the incursion of "non-art" into hallowed gallery confines — surely affirm the vitality of current art practice and the art gallery just as surely as they challenge their exclusivity in the social, cultural and urban fabric.

At their best, museums and galleries reinvent themselves over time, through evolving collections, through dialogue with artists and communities, and through reappraisal and realignment of what they do and how they do it. MUSEOPATHY stands as a milestone for the Agnes Etherington Art Centre not only for its ambition, quality and intelligence, but also because it has called on us to address these sometimes elusive goals. For that, I salute its curators, its artists, collaborating institutions, lenders and supporters. I hope they will look back on the event with pride, just as I look forward to the new challenges and opportunities it has helped create.

Janet M. Brooke
Director

INTRODUCTION

Jan Allen

MUSEOPATHY IS A MULTI-SITE EXHIBITION in museums and heritage sites throughout Kingston, a city with an unusually rich mix of specialist museums reflecting its military, political, marine, and corrections histories and less well-known venues dedicated to geology, health care, and ice hockey. Presented by the Agnes Etherington Art Centre in the summer of 2001, the project consisted of visual artists' installations of site-specific works in museums and, during the same period, an exhibition of objects from the collections of the city's museums was featured at the Art Centre.

Inspired by city-wide, multi-site projects in Europe and by the potential to reach new audiences by placing contemporary art in non-traditional settings, I invited the curatorial team Jim Drobnick and Jennifer Fisher (a.k.a. DisplayCult) to curate an exhibition that would commission artists to install site-responsive artworks in museums across the city. It was a task they undertook with great energy and imagination.

Drobnick and Fisher complemented the artists' installations with an exhibition of works from the collections of participating museums. This exciting model of reciprocity — art into museums and museum collections into the gallery — generated multiple points of access to the show and a dynamic interpretive field. The resulting display in the Samuel J. Zacks and Contemporary Feature Galleries of the Art Centre was entitled COLLECTIONEERING. The exhibition made use of what Drobnick and Fisher describe (after Walter Benjamin) as constellatory epistemology as an organizing principle of display.

An additional aspect of the project was produced by DisplayCult: EMPATHOLOGY consisted of performance works by four artists, Diane Borsato, Peter Hobbs, Linda Montano and Clive Robertson. The first three were presented to audiences at museum sites on the opening day of MUSEOPATHY, while Robertson's piece took place weekly through the run of the exhibition. These engaging and incisive works brought a dynamic presence to the project that vitally extended the experience of the whole.

This publication documents the project and presents a text by Drobnick and Fisher elaborating their curatorial framework and its implicit analysis of display.

They offer a lively account of the complex of components of MUSEOPATHY, including artists' museum interventions, the COLLECTIONEERING display and EMPATHOLOGY.

It was a pleasure and privilege to work with Jim Drobnick and Jennifer Fisher on the development and implementation of this exhibition. Their infectious enthusiasm for the possibilities of this project and their enormous commitment to its successful realization galvanized all those involved. I thank them for the exceptional quality of their work and their capacity to think above, beyond, and around all apparent obstacles.

My heartfelt thanks likewise go to the directors, curators and staff of participating museums. Their willingness to take risks, to engage with the conceptual and technical challenges of MUSEOPATHY and to generously support its development despite already stretched time and resources are deeply appreciated. Kingston should be very proud of the quality and unstinting dedication of its museum community.

MUSEOPATHY required exceptional efforts on the part of Art Centre staff at every step. My special thanks are extended to Pat Sullivan, Michelle Hynes, Barry Fagan and to Nigel Barnett and his installation crew. I also thank the remarkably capable curatorial assistants who worked on this project: Donna Gillespie, Steven Stowell, Julie Fiala and York Lethbridge. Deep appreciation goes to Art Centre Director David McTavish for his early encouragement and sustained support of the exhibition and to Acting Director Dorothy Farr for moral support and practical assistance throughout.

The artists were — without exception — generous, innovative and incisive: they engaged with the details of research into prospective sites, development of proposals and on-site installation with good humour and imagination. The variety and quality of the resulting works attest to the vigour of their response to the challenges of this project. Many thanks to: John Dickson, Fastwürms (Kim Kozzi and Dai Skuse), Jamelie Hassan, Barb Hunt, Brian Jungen, Komar and Melamid / William McClelland, Anne Ramsden, Mitch Robertson, and Mel Ziegler. It was a pleasure to have Joyce Wieland (1931–1998) represented in this project: appropriately, she was an artist who made a virtue of crossing disciplinary boundaries. Special gratitude is extended to performance artists Diane Borsato, Peter Hobbs, Linda Montano and Clive Robertson for their memorable contributions.

GUEST CURATORS' ACKNOWLEDGMENTS

Jim Drobnick and Jennifer Fisher

A COMPLEX AND AMBITIOUS PROJECT LIKE MUSEOPATHY can only occur with the dedicated involvement of a large number of individuals.

Our profound thanks go to the artists — Diane Borsato, John Dickson, Fastwürms, Jamelie Hassan, Peter Hobbs, Barb Hunt, Brian Jungen, Vitaly Komar and Alexander Melamid, William McClelland, Linda Montano, Anne Ramsden, Clive Robertson, Mitch Robertson and Mel Ziegler — for their enthusiastic participation, skilful installation, and thought-provoking performances and artworks. We were delighted to present Joyce Wieland's work, with the cooperation of the Canadian Filmmakers' Distribution Centre.

The principal host for this project, the Agnes Etherington Art Centre, made a courageous commitment and offered generous support during the three years it took to research, organize and manifest the exhibition. We are especially thankful to Jan Allen, Curator of Contemporary Art, who invited us as guest curators. She worked tirelessly to facilitate the many demands of this project and contributed extraordinary efforts in regard to fundraising, administration, promotion, technical assistance, and coordination among the participating museums. Her resourcefulness, adroit planning and unwavering encouragement were essential to the success of MUSEOPATHY.

David McTavish, former Director of the Art Centre, and Dorothy Farr, Barry Fagan, Pat Sullivan and Michelle Hynes provided solid backing and a welcoming environment for the project. Integral to resolving many challenging details were curatorial assistants Julie Fiala and R.J. York Lethbridge. We appreciated the talents of Nigel Barnett and his installation team, Amanda Happé, Maureen Sheridan, Aida Sulcs-McDonald and Scott Wallis. Thanks are also extended to those who impeccably DJ'ed the broadcasting of *Call to Art* throughout the summer: Courtney Barry, Robin Chung, Jennifer Radford Gibson, Annabel Hanson and Grace Lee. In 1999 and 2000, curatorial assistants Donna Gillespie and Steven F. Stowell gathered useful preliminary research for the show.

It was a distinct pleasure for us to work with the directors, curators and staff of the museums and heritage sites of Kingston. We were impressed by their abundant hospitality, openness to creative ideas and passionate devotion to their institutions. They warmly invited us into their archives and collections, freely shared their interests and knowledge, loaned us many intriguing objects and offered their spaces wholeheartedly to the presence of MUSEOPATHY and EMPATHOLOGY artists. We wish to thank Donna Lusk, John Coleman and Mark Peters at Bellevue House National Historic Site; Dave St. Onge at the Correctional Service of Canada Museum; Ed Grenda at the International Ice Hockey Federation Museum and the Murney Tower National Historic Site; Maurice Smith and Susan Corbett-Cyr at the Marine Museum of the Great Lakes at Kingston; Mark Badham at the Miller Museum of Geology and Mineralogy; Dr. James Low, Heather Blythe and Rona Rustige at the Museum of Health Care at Kingston; and Ross McKenzie at the Royal Military College of Canada Museum. We also greatly appreciate the help of all of the volunteers, guides and summer staff, such as Mary-Kathleen Donn, Rebecca Martin and Kathleen Raddon, who attended to the artworks and thoughtfully explained their intricacies to visitors.

We thank Barbara Fischer for her insightful reading of the show presented at the public forum. And we are grateful to all those whose skill, talent and friendship benefited MUSEOPATHY in numerous ways: Teena Aujla, Renee Baert, Rodolfo Borello, Joan Borsa, Dean Baldwin, Ron Benner, Jerry Browne, Jennifer deFreitas, Nikki Forrest, Lisa Germany, John Grenville, Lisa LaFrance, Francis Leeming, Paul Litherland, Chris Peck, Aaron Pollard, Jocelyn Purdie, Kim Sawchuk, Kitty Scott, Jean Spence, Karen Trask, and Jessica Wyman.

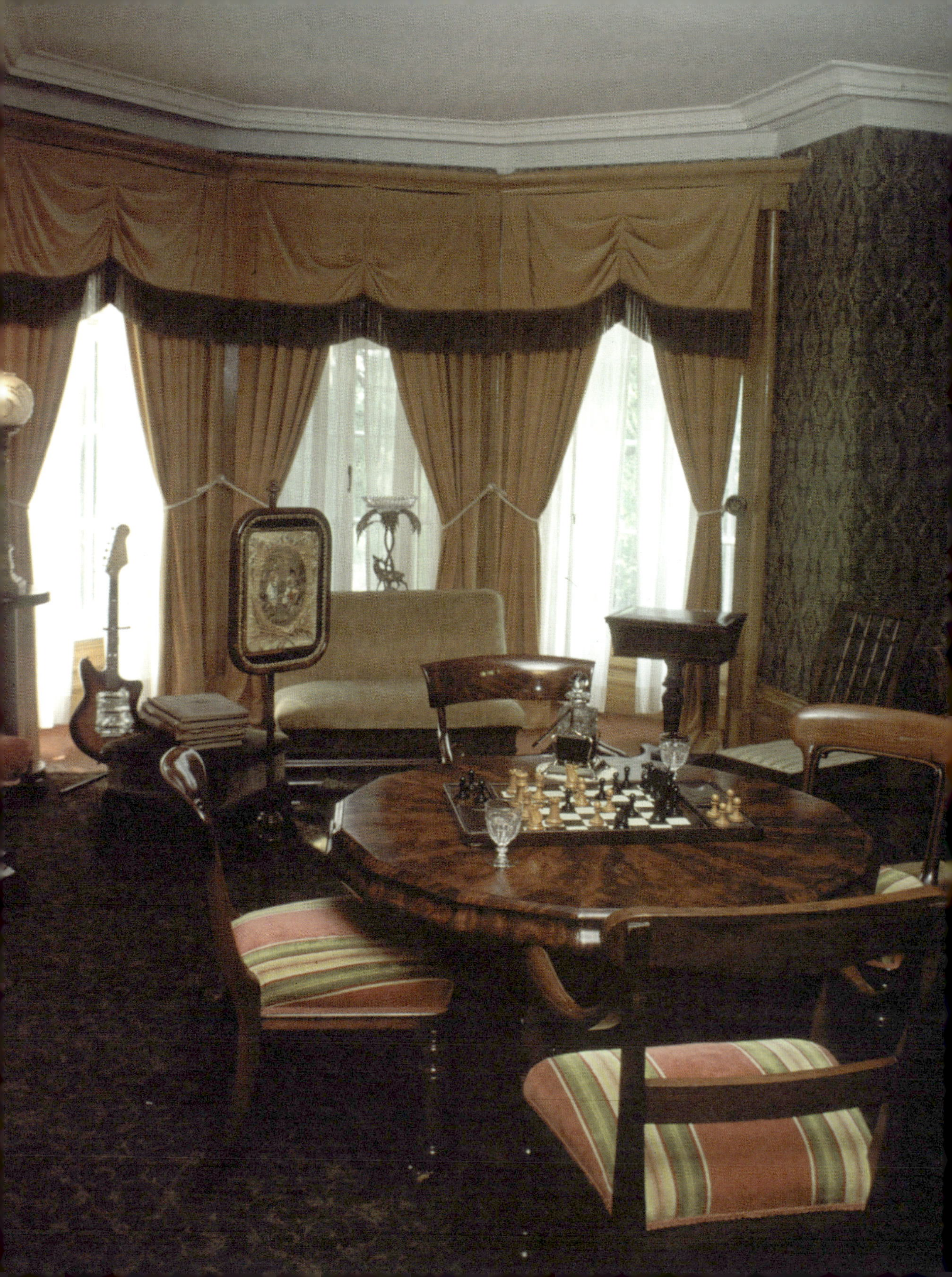

MUSEOPATHY

Jim Drobnick and Jennifer Fisher

MUSEUMS ARE NOT SIMPLY REPOSITORIES; they are also sites for creative endeavour. MUSEOPATHY evolved out of DisplayCult's ongoing engagement with redefining notions of the aesthetic and commitment to experimenting with exhibition prototypes. While the nascent genre of museum intervention has provided a number of examples of how museum discourses can be deconstructed, our project also encompassed the extra-discursive aspects of the museal and posed the museum in both its experiential aspects and generative capacities.

For a project like this to materialize, a significant collaborative network had to be organized linking the eclectic museums and heritage sites existing throughout Kingston. Our concept for the overall project of MUSEOPATHY pivoted on cultivating a reciprocating dynamic, one which involved three interrelated parts. We first invited ten artists (or artist groups) to create site-specific interventions in museums around the city. At the same time, we commissioned four performance artists to stage events with artifacts and audiences under the title EMPATHOLOGY. The third component, COLLECTIONEERING, exhibited objects borrowed from the city's museum collections and arranged by us in a postmodern *wunderkammer* at the Agnes Etherington Art Centre. Just as artworks and performance artists were installed in non-art museums, objects from historical sites and museums were restaged in a contemporary art space. The cumulative effect of these curatorial interventions and resituations interrogated the conventions of display, inquired into the dynamics of collecting, and initiated a reframing of Kingston's material culture.

Mel Ziegler, installation view, *Mail Order Authenticity* 2001

The neologism of the title, MUSEOPATHY, pertains first to "museo-," the museum. The suffix "-pathy" evokes two related ideas: that of "moving" and "being moved." In one sense the suffix alludes to the *path*ways that link the citywide components of the show, the peregrinations of the audience from site to site, and the many exchanges that occurred between artists, artworks and artifacts. In another sense, the meaning of "-pathy" stems from its etymological origin — the Greek word for "emotion" or "feeling" and the root of words such as "pathos." Rather than focus on the museum as something pathological, we premised MUSEOPATHY on a logic of homeopathy in which "like treats like" and each artist, to some degree, mimicked aspects of museum display.

MUSEOPATHY explored the implications of museological affect — how museums feel and subtly influence visitors. The auratic features of museums — their particular moods, presences, ambiances — were highlighted, intensified or counteracted in order to examine meanings that may have been lost due to the exigencies of conveying persuasive, singular narratives. Our impetus was to foreground the great diversity of relational experiences within a civic exhibitionary complex rather than a pure aesthetic gaze upon discrete, autonomous objects. This emphasis on immersed beholding requires the apprehension of the overall reality of the display context, one that goes beyond reading an exhibition as if it were a linear text. MUSEOPATHY thus focused on the types of affective interactions that take place in museums, such as between audiences and objects, between objects and the collections, and among the varied exhibition contexts of Kingston as a whole.

None of the artworks or performances could be viewed in isolation. Either they were seen after visitors passed through the host's site and collections, or they were covertly integrated into the architecture and displays. These projects developed modes of connecting conscious and unconscious links; they hitched rides, as it were, on the museums' spaces and auratic qualities. Rather than presenting a fixed set of meanings, the artists' interventions incorporated museal ambiance into the artworks themselves and introduced into the museums a dialectical present of unstable and unreconciled realities. Aesthetic sensibility thus operated as a means by which "feelings" accompany the processes of "coming to know," linking pathic and epistemological modalities. While such precognitive sensations as mood or presence may not be inherently meaningful in the sense of being articulated by language, they nevertheless contribute to critical awareness and political discernment.[1]

Every display venue, whether an art gallery, heritage site or living history museum, addresses its audience via particular modes of exhibition architecture, ambulation, information, object arrangement and *mise-en-scène*. The past decade has witnessed the increased prominence of the innovative genre of museum intervention that specifically targets such collection and display dynamics. "Museum intervention" is the term used to describe the collaboration between artists and institutions to transform the museum from a *container* of cultural artifacts to a *medium* of contemporary work. In this practice, the museum context becomes the raw material or "cultural readymade"[2] for artistic analysis, commentary and reconfiguration.

Museum interventions in the past century have originated from a multitude of aesthetic tactical positions, from the covert and surreptitious to the confrontational and iconoclastic. The benign interventions of Pierre Bonnard, for instance, who clandestinely entered museums with a brush and palette to make minute alterations to his paintings, contrast markedly with the radicality of F.T. Marinetti's exhortations about the obsolescence of museums and the need to burn them down altogether. Between such extremes lie a number of strategies that seek to appropriate, critique, reform and revitalize the museum. Artists have acted as curators and rearranged displays, unlocked storage rooms and offices, inhabited the museum's galleries, interacted with museumgoers, articulated alternative histories and identities, subverted authoritative hierarchies, and exposed the social, political and ideological underpinnings of the museum as an institution. Museum interventions, such as those of Fred Wilson, Joseph Kosuth, Sophie Calle and N.E. Thing, Co., to name just a few, have introduced artworks that rupture the assumed objectivity and universality of exhibition narratives, and cunningly create anxieties and unexpected encounters. In short, these interventions scrutinize the processes by which society sacralizes cultural products, turning sites of consolidation and preservation into ones of dialogue and contestation.[3]

The three components of MUSEOPATHY, EMPATHOLOGY and COLLECTIONEERING build upon DisplayCult's continuing investigation into practices of display and collecting.[4] When conversing with Jan Allen, Curator of Contemporary Art, about a project we had just completed involving museum intervention (produced in collaboration with Jamelie Hassan at Eldon House, a museum and historic site in London[5]), a common interest was forged. Museum interventions have occurred in high-profile institutions in Europe and America, and Jan proposed that Kingston's fascinating array of heritage museums would be ideal for a project in this genre. At her invitation, we found the city's many compelling sites a fertile ground for researching, theorizing and ultimately curating an exhibition and series of interventions and performances.

Several criteria guided our selection of artists for the installations of MUSEOPATHY and the performances of EMPATHOLOGY. We invited artists who utilized intervention and site-specificity consistently in their work. Other artists struck our interest because they had created their own, albeit temporary, personal museums. A few had addressed the concept of the museum or practices of collecting, while others engaged with collecting in a more general sense by working in the series or multiple format. We paired the artists with the institutions, in many cases letting the artists decide which site had the most resonance for their work. As well, the artists utilized a myriad of media, including video, audio, sculpture, fibres, painting, photography, performance, multiples and text, as well as working with landscape and architectural elements. The aesthetic strategies ranged from the sensational to the discreet — such that no viewer could assume the same approach would be in effect when travelling from site to site.

Despite the similar task of inquiring into the logic and affect of the host museums, collections and displays, the interventions were remarkably varied, encompassing playful, personal, pedagogical, or polemical methodologies. Artists directly responded to specific artifacts at their sites by recontextualizing them in new arrangements, mimicking their production, or trying to glean information from them in unusual ways. Artists also created masquerade objects or inserted obvious fakes into the displays — which raised questions about authenticity, historical veracity and believability. Several of the museums retain traces of their former existence as residences or places of work, and returning a living presence to these sites motivated artists to intervene in personal ways by sharing relevant aspects of their own lives or by imagining fictive characters to humanize the space. There is an inherent performativity to the act of attending museums, and some artists foregrounded the sacralizing rituals and potential for transformation that exists whenever a visit is undertaken. Acknowledging the fact that during the summer months in Kingston many museumgoers are engaging in leisure pursuits, the thematics of recreation and tourism were emphasized. Artist-made postcards, souvenirs, pamphlets and other items were often available to pick up or purchase. The museum and heritage sites hosting MUSEOPATHY and EMPATHOLOGY are more than intriguing backdrops for artistic intervention; they are also active agents in the public sphere. An interest in the public dimension of these sites — their grounds, façades, signage and acoustic qualities — infused a number of the artists' projects, thus influencing the everyday life of the city beyond the specific parameters of the exhibition itself.

Besides preserving the historical and material culture of Kingston, the institutions participating in this project also serve as hubs of social activity for a wide range of clubs, groups and associations. While a broad community of people invest their time and efforts toward supporting the museums, large numbers also utilize them as meeting places, training grounds or symbolic centres. We found a vital sense of community at each MUSEOPATHY site — whether in terms of the original users or residents of the buildings, the groups of people and their efforts which are represented in the displays, or the workers who presently maintain and animate the sites. The sense of community derived from several factors: strong group coherence (cadets, hockey teams, sailors), professional identities (doctors, nurses, geologists, art patrons), committed enthusiasts (amateur historians, hobbyists) and, especially, devoted staff at all of the sites.[6]

Many of the artists in MUSEOPATHY and EMPATHOLOGY were influenced by the subcultural elements of the sites. Not only did they address the presence of communities in the orientation and subject matter of their interventions, they also based their works upon pertinent aspects of their own personal interests beyond the realm of art. For instance, Fastwürms revealed their rockhounding activities; Mitch Robertson drew upon his childhood years as a hockey player; Jamelie Hassan acknowledged her experience as a medical caregiver and mother; and John Dickson exposed an affinity with model boatbuilders and scuba divers.

The multi-functionality of Kingston's museum sites reflects in many ways their complex social history and layered genealogy of use. Every artist recognized that viewing art may not have been a primary orientation in sites devoted to historical and educational pursuits. This led several interventions to factor in the diverse interests of their audiences. Mel Ziegler, for instance, implicitly addressed home decorators and antique collectors, Barb Hunt military and peacekeeping personnel, and Diane Borsato cadets and alumni from the Royal Military College.

Situated in contexts not "engineered" or "determined" to display art, MUSEOPATHY and EMPATHOLOGY's interventions created unanticipated aesthetic experiences. An element of surprise permeated the works, and revelation or shock could potentially disturb conventional museumgoing. From their interior position, artists adopted and modulated the voice of "museum" authority. Formulating parallel utterances to the narratives of the host museums, the interventions posed alternative truths and foregrounded both the museum's taxonomies and its mood.

This is not to say, however, that the interventions appealed only to art cognoscenti. Most, if not all, of the interventions deliberately sought to connect with non-art audiences. A few turned into noted photo-opportunities. Some, like those by Diane Borsato, Fastwürms, Linda Montano and Clive Robertson, were friendly, approachable, even conversational at times. Barb Hunt and Komar & Melamid employed beautiful and sonorous experiences respectively to capture attention. A few artists, such as Mitch Robertson and Mel Ziegler, absorbed visitors in a game-like fashion, testing their knowledge and perceptivity. Offering perplexing or enigmatic objects, texts or images, as presented by Brian Jungen, John Dickson, Anne Ramsden or Joyce Wieland, challenged beholders to interpret and divine meaning. On the more extreme edge, works by Peter Hobbs and Jamelie Hassan confronted viewers with emotional or corporeal intensities that forced a reckoning with the sometimes difficult realities of death and birth.[7]

Ultimately, MUSEOPATHY and EMPATHOLOGY's focus on the act of intervention emphasized the performative nature of museum visits. Combining museums, artists, audiences, ephemeral installations, shifting meanings, and a demanding perambulatory itinerary across the city, the project as a whole defined a Kingstonian version of the "grand tour" whereby the network and accumulation of experiences was just as important as any individual artwork or site. Collaborating with many of Kingston's renowned museum and heritage sites, MUSEOPATHY interrogated the ways in which objects, images and buildings are utilized in a city's self-representation. By involving a wide variety of institutions, a discussion was created about the general meanings and practices of collecting, display and museal experience. By merging art and artifacts in a mutual relationship, the project crossed disciplinary boundaries and inspired a dialogue between traditionally separate domains of aesthetics, history, popular culture, science and other fields. By occupying a series of museums at the same time, MUSEOPATHY performed a catalytic role in re-experiencing the sweep of material culture in Kingston's cityscape.

NOTES

1. Recent scholarship has recuperated the aesthetic as a form of critical cognition. See, for example, Susan Buck-Morss, "Aesthetics and Anaesthetics: Walter Benjamin's Artwork Essay Reconsidered," *October* 62, Fall 1992; and Terry Eagleton, *The Ideology of the Aesthetic*, Oxford: Basil and Blackwood Ltd., 1990.

2. This term was used by Barbara Fischer in her presentation at the forum for MUSEOPATHY, Kingston, June 24, 2001.

3. MUSEOPATHY and EMPATHOLOGY raise a number of theoretical issues that exceed our available space. For readers interested in museum intervention, some useful sources include: A.A. Bronson and Peggy Gale, eds., *Museums by Artists*, Toronto: Art Metropole, 1983; Lisa G. Corrin, ed., *Mining the Museum: An Installation by Fred Wilson*, New York & Baltimore: The New Press and The Contemporary, 1994; Neil Cummings and Marysia Lewandowska, *The Value of Things*, Basel, Boston, Berlin: Birkhäuser, 2000; *The Desire of the Museum*, New York: Whitney Museum of American Art, 1989; Ivan Karp and Steven D. Lavine, eds., *Exhibiting Cultures: The Poetics and Politics of Museum Display*, Washington: Smithsonian, 1991; Kynaston McShine, *The Museum as Muse: Artists Reflect*, New York: The Museum of Modern Art, 1999; James Putnam, *Art and Artifact: Museum as Medium*, London: Thames & Hudson, 2001; Ingrid Schaffner and Mathias Winzen, eds., *Deep Storage: Collecting, Storing and Archiving in Art*, Munich & New York: Prestel, 1998. Nearly contemporaneous with MUSEOPATHY, the exhibition *Give & Take* curated by Lisa Corrin explored similar themes. See *Give & Take*, London: Serpentine Gallery, 2001.

4. On collecting, see, e.g., Jennifer Fisher, *Aesthetic Contingencies: Relational Enactments in Display Culture*, Ph.D. Dissertation, Montreal: Concordia University, 1995; on display practices, see our recent catalogue, *CounterPoses*, Montreal: DisplayCult and Oboro, 2002, and our forthcoming anthology, *Living Display*, Chicago: University of Chicago Press.

5. See our text on "The Servant Problem" and Hassan's curatorial premise in Jamelie Hassan, ed., *Trespassers & Captives*, London, ON: London Regional Art and Historical Museums, 2000.

6. This vital sense of community was represented in COLLECTIONEERING by two walls of group photographs associated with the MUSEOPATHY sites. Spanning historical and contemporary eras, these photographs of graduations, commemorative views of staff, and historical groupings captured six generations of Kingstonians living, studying and working in the city.

7. In the following pages, artists' comments are integrated into our descriptions and interpretations of their works.

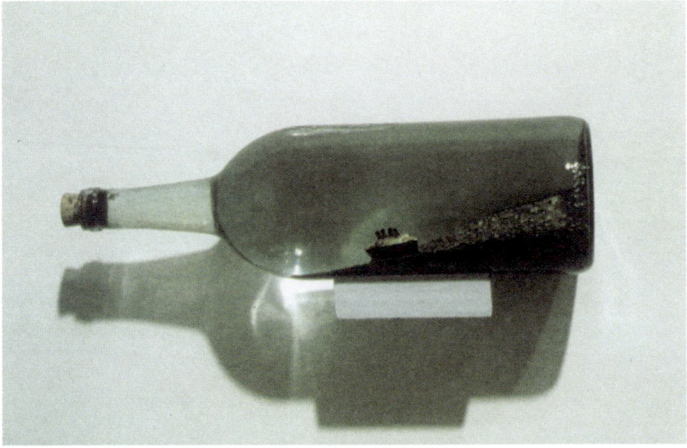

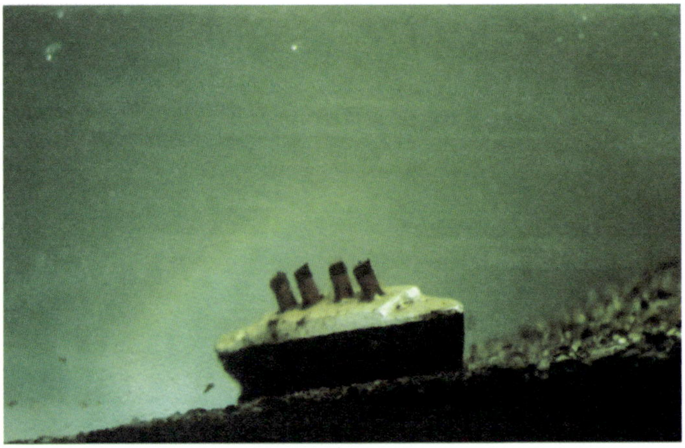

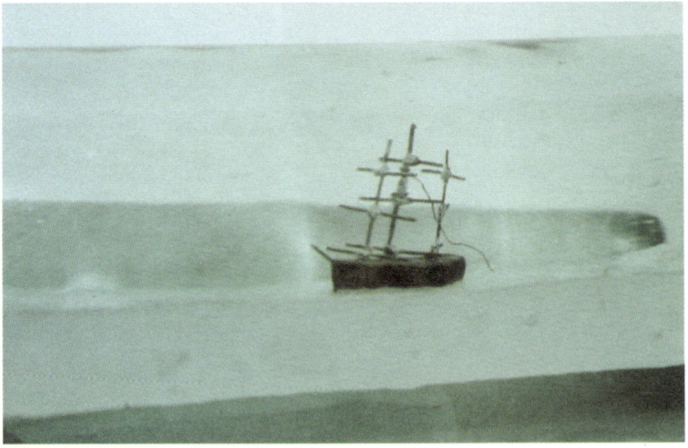

John Dickson, *Ten Small Nautical Disasters* 1996–97
(top: *Titanic*; centre: *Titanic* detail; bottom: *Franklin Expedition*)

JOHN DICKSON

Marine Museum of the Great Lakes at Kingston

WATER, IN ALL OF ITS VARIETIES AND MANIFESTATIONS, has preoccupied John Dickson throughout his career. His artworks have explored the complex dynamics of this elemental fluid as both a natural and cultural phenomenon, with both mundane and sublime implications, such as can be found in tears, plumbing, hygiene and ecological cycles. For MUSEOPATHY, he focused on the more sensational notions of life at sea and the popular fascination with extreme oceanic phenomena.

His installations at the Marine Museum implicitly drew upon Kingston's past as a strategically important naval base during the eighteenth and nineteenth centuries when Britain and France struggled over the possession of North America. Once a centre of shipbuilding and repair, Kingston is now known for its shipwrecks and underwater diving. The Marine Museum enshrines an abundance of the Great Lakes' material heritage, and the adjacent drydock, designated a National Historic Site, preserves a link to the era of nautical prestige. Dickson, who grew up Kingston, bears a longstanding affinity with the sensibility of the lake and its cultural role in the life of city.

Dickson sited his work both inside and on the grounds of the museum. In the Sail and Steam Gallery, he installed a selection from *Ten Small Nautical Disasters*, a series directly drawing from the "ship in the bottle" genre. This popular nautical folk art involves the skilful crafting of perfectly scaled ships mysteriously ensconced within transparent bottles. Typically, the themes represented are nostalgic reflections upon life at sea and paeans to human mastery over the elements. Dickson, however, displaced such romantic and celebratory notions with tragic and cautionary scenes. While the artist maintained the tradition of painstaking and inventive craftsmanship (he carved the lilliputian boats out of cork, affixing them with magnets), viewers studied tiny tableaux of historic and legendary catastrophes such as the Franklin Expedition fatefully frozen in polar ice, the *Titanic* confronted by an

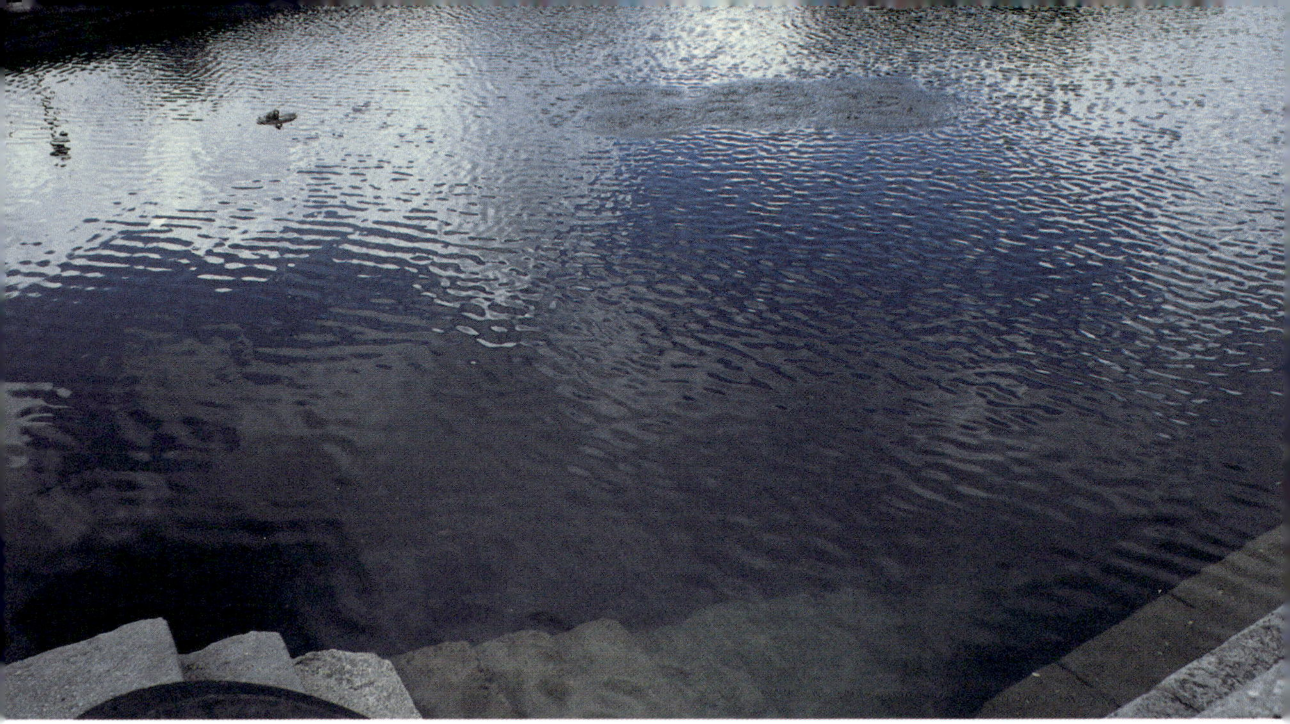

John Dickson, *SOS* 2001

ominous iceberg, the oil tanker *Exxon Valdez* spilling its devastating cargo, and the sea monster Leviathan heralding over a heap of shipwrecks. The miniaturization rendered pelagic calamities tangible and psychically manageable, as well as darkly humorous.

Dickson's interventions were subtle and stealthy. Positioned in museum-like cases, *Nautical Disasters* existed alongside examples of model shipbuilding and operated in continuity with the museum's displays of marine technology and relics. *Cyclone*, similarly, mimicked interactive exhibits nearby. A tall ship floated calmly in a twenty-litre glass bottle moored in a dark wooden cabinet. Beholders pushed a button to propel the bottle and its contents into a noisy spin. As the vortex gathered momentum and white sand swirled upwards, the boat helplessly listed and rotated. Even though the mechanism was controlled by viewers, who could entertain the idea that the beleaguered craft bobbed turbulently at their whim, *Cyclone*, like *Nautical Disasters*, conveyed how the unpredictable power of natural forces often reduces human pride to folly.

Outside the museum, situated in the still waters of the drydock, was a work that Dickson, appropriate to the diving activity at the site, installed wearing wetsuit and snorkel. Every twenty-two seconds, bubbles rose from the murky medium, broke

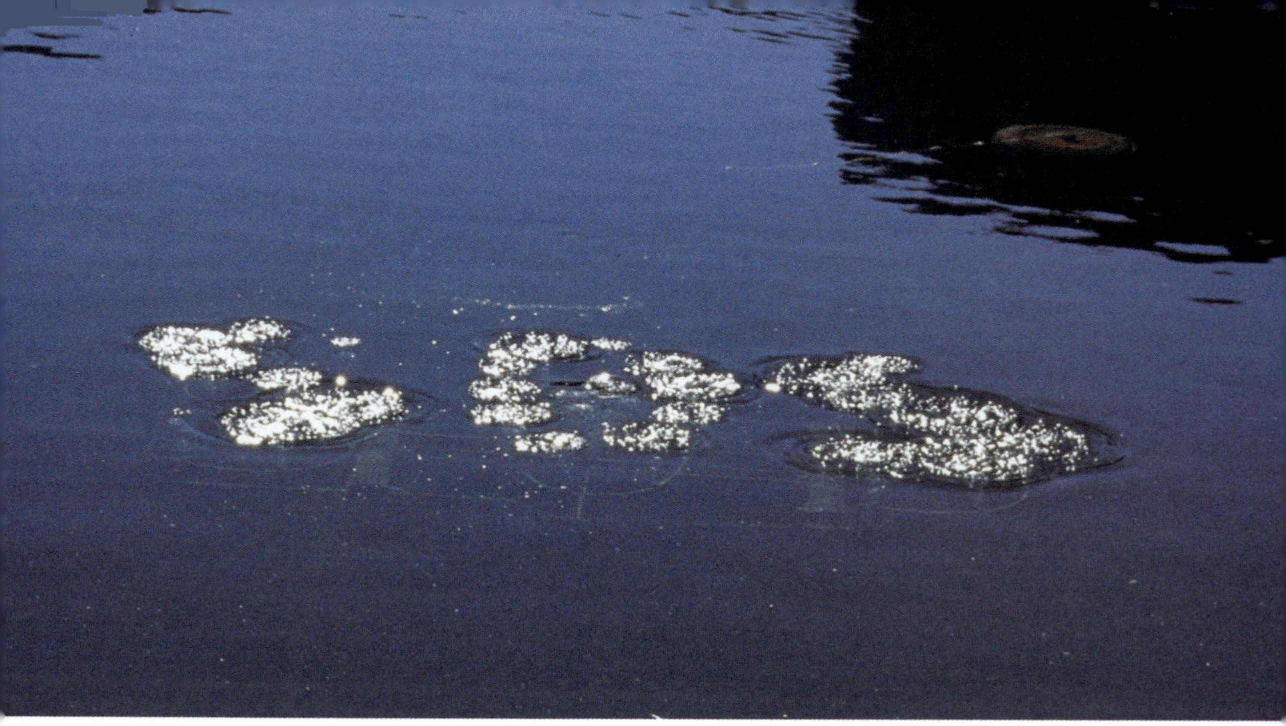

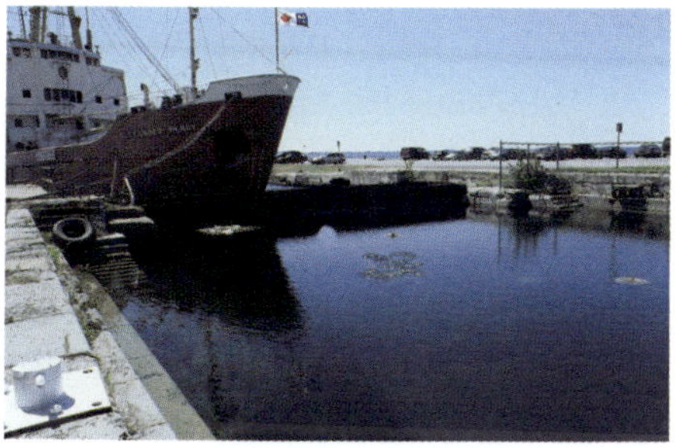

Drydock, Marine Museum

the surface and coalesced to form the letters "SOS." In the fluid darkness lay an anchored apparatus of copper tubes and solenoid valves, rigged to a compressor and timed to release the urgent call again and again throughout the day. While the message of the letters was clear, the identity of the sender remained cryptic. Was it a marooned ship, a submerged diver in distress, or a personification of the lake itself? Given the prevalence of tragedy in marine history and the plethora of shipwrecks in the Kingston area, "save our souls" could be fathomed as the beseeching of restless underwater ghosts. But an environmental emergency also resonated in *SOS*'s terse communication, one in which Lake Ontario, which is in danger of dying, was figuratively given a voice. The drydock itself is an unfortunate example of such ecological challenges, since effluent from years of shipbuilding has accumulated into sludge at the bottom; to disturb it is to unleash a toxic black plume. During the summer, Dickson's bubbly missive had the strange, unintended effect of attracting floating debris (by breaking the water's surface tension), underscoring further the exigency of the lake's continuing predicament.

FASTWÜRMS

Miller Museum of Geology and Mineralogy, Queen's University

IN FASTWÜRMS' OEUVRE, NATURE IS OFTEN POSITIONED as the "other" to modern technological society. Building upon earlier artworks that addressed crystal worship, landscape symbolism, territorial politics, and environmentalist concerns, their installation at the Miller Museum of Geology and Mineralogy engaged with the myriad forms of rock collecting and appreciation — or what we call *geophilia* — that can be found not only in museums, but also in souvenir merchandising, hobby clubs, cartoons and fanzines.

The museum's exquisite array of antique oak cabinets, systematically displaying thousands of mineral specimens, and educational dioramas delineating the evolution of the earth and its life forms, provided an apt context for Kim Kozzi and

Fastwürms, detail, *Ms. Rockhound 2001* 2001

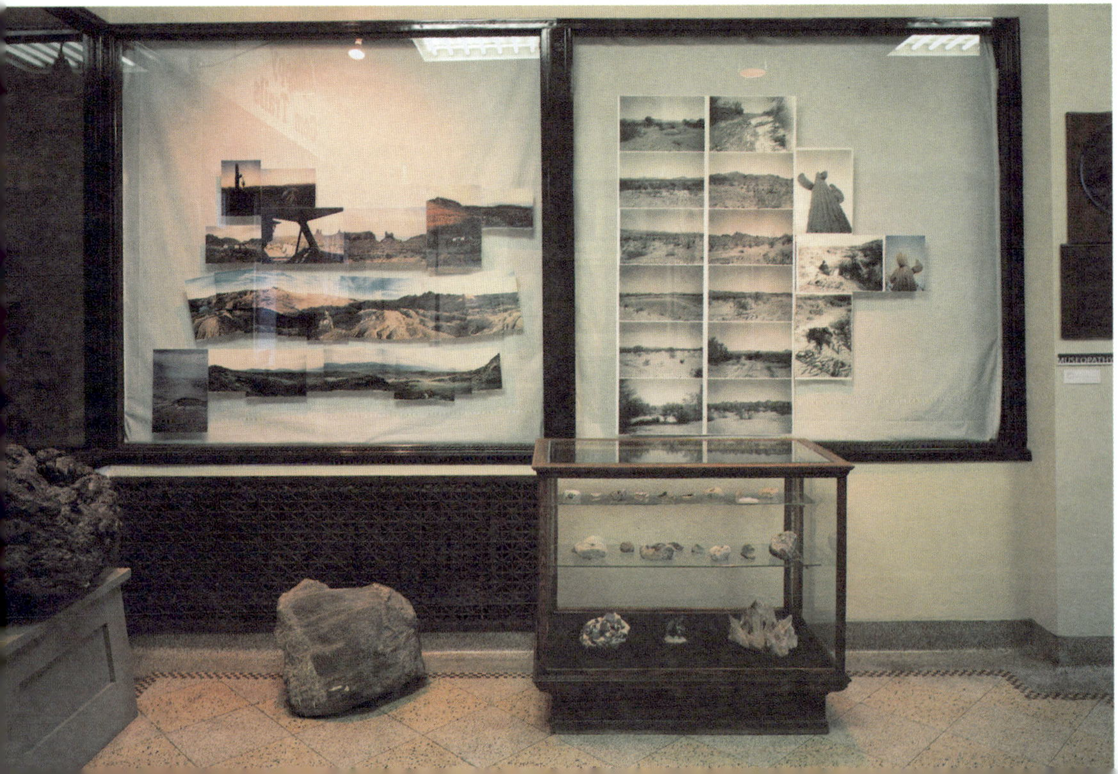

Dai Skuse, themselves mineralogical enthusiasts. Their geological passions were presented within the bricolage aesthetics of a rockhound convention booth combining a manic diversity of presentation styles: documentary photographs, digital prints, ink drawings, handmade signs and maps, as well as vitrines full of "artistically" altered rocks. Contrary to minimalist earthworks like Smithson's dialectical site/non-sites, which drew upon geology as an authoritative discipline, Fastwürms' *Ms. Rockhound 2001* extolled the virtues of amateurism and geophilia in popular and even "trash" cultural contexts.

A hand-painted sign reading "Welcome Rockhounds" greeted visitors as they entered the museum. The left wall displayed panoramas of Fastwürms' geological sojourn to the American Southwest. Camping in desert landscapes, admiring sunset views and rugged canyons, these photographs documented an actual rockhounding trip (one not originally intended as art) to Kofa, Arizona, and travels across the continent to Mount Ida, Death Valley, the Badlands and Blind River. It was a field trip common to geology students. Further documentation included a contour map of North America with rock samples gathered on the trip keyed to geographical points with strands of colourful yarn, like an amateur science fair exhibit. The deliberately naive presentation belied the artists' serious appreciation of geology; theirs is an insider's humour recognizing that the motivation of many professional scientists originates in childhood obsessions.

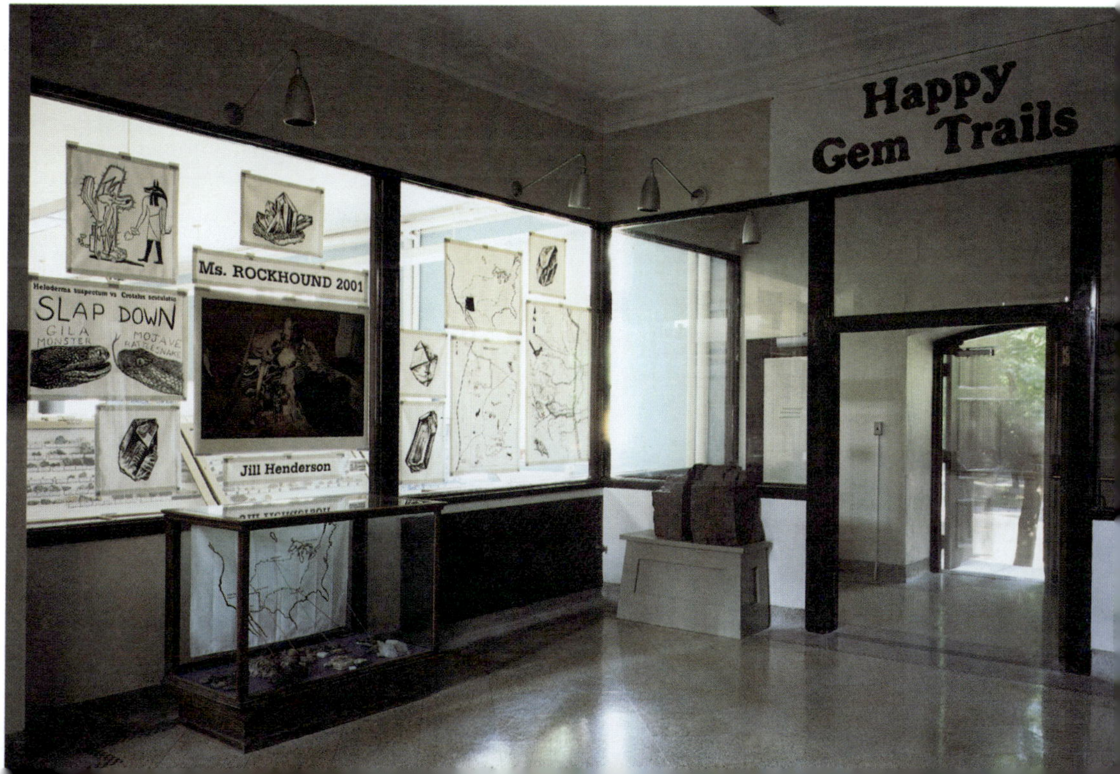

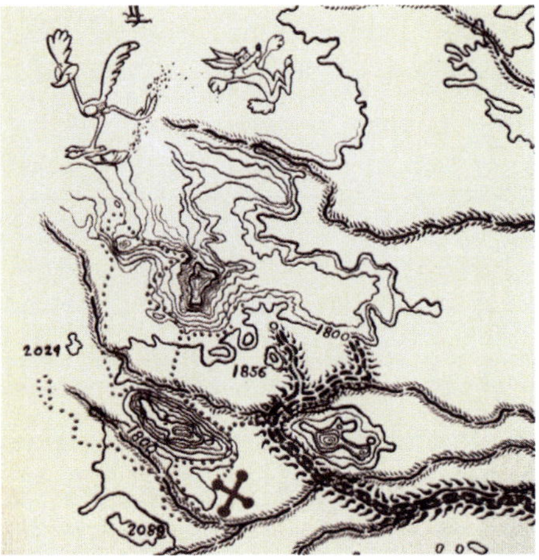

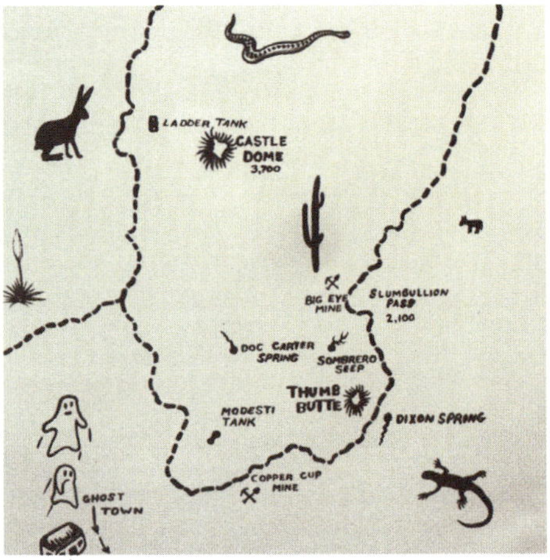

The opposite wall featured the reverberations of geophilia in popular culture. Maps and drawings playfully imitated the folky illustrations of independent rock-hound publications such as *Gem Trails* field guides. Fastwürms' maps were full of corny icons: picks and shovels to indicate mines, ghosts marking abandoned towns, and x's demarcating interesting rock finds, along with elevation lines, cactus silhouettes and longhorn skulls. These pictographic representations evidenced the confidence of 'zine do-it-yourselfers in legitimizing their own experience and knowledge. The rudimentary maps also hinted at the excitement of speculation by which even raw landscapes are infused with cultural significance.

Animals figure prominently in Fastwürms' iconography, and their bestiary here included such local southwestern fauna as roadrunners, lizards and snakes. A poster spoofing Wrestlemania advertised an upcoming "slap down" match between a gila monster and a rattlesnake. Another drawing depicted Wile E. Coyote confronting Anubis, the jackal-headed Egyptian god of the dead. The ludic confrontations between the carnivalesque and the mythological, the cartoonish and the environmental, the terrestrial and nether worlds, revealed the numerous ways in which nature is corralled into serving human interests, whether for entertainment or cosmological explanation.

In a similar vein, the mineral and the zoomorphic unnaturally mixed in a vitrine displaying the "life of rocks" — stones fitted with taxidermy glass eyes. Looking at beholders with single, double and triple eyes, these lumpish entities expressed forlorn, cute, mutant or bewitching countenances. Such lithic animism recalls vitalist philosophies that often adhere to stones and crystals. Fastwürms parodied

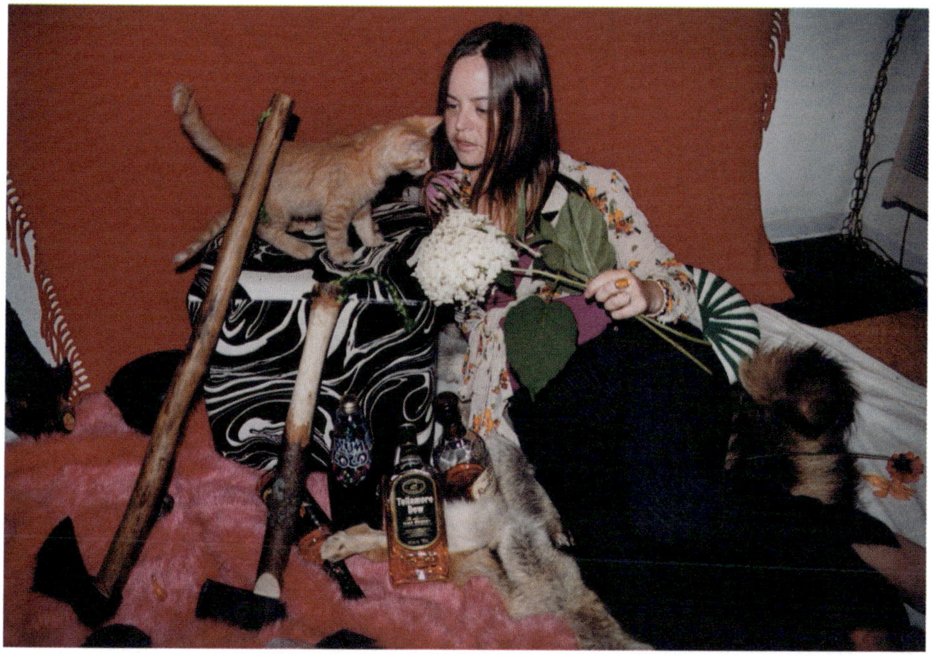

the pet rocks, kitschy paper weights, and artsy gifts pervading grade-school projects, craft fairs, head shops and New Age emporia while simultaneously tapping into the geophilic community of the lapidary club that meets in the Geological Sciences building. And a sign directing visitors to "Mark's Rock Shop" incorporated the museum's curator, Mark Badham, in the installation: one can determine his presence by the posting of "in" or "out" options.

The cynosure of Fastwürms' convention-style display was a large photographic portrait of "Ms. Rockhound 2001" holding a bouquet and reclining upon swatches of fur. Amidst axes and half-empty liquor bottles, artist Jill Henderson modelled as the poster girl for the meeting of academic and youth cultures, hard science and hard partying. The youthful appearance of the 31-year-old friend of the artists spoke to the tradition of informal festivities and student photography. Getting "stoned" and taking "trips" assumed more than just geological meanings. Rockhounding, university education, even museum visits, Fastwürms implied, are acts of discovery where the focus on "getting there" is just as significant as what might be found upon arrival.

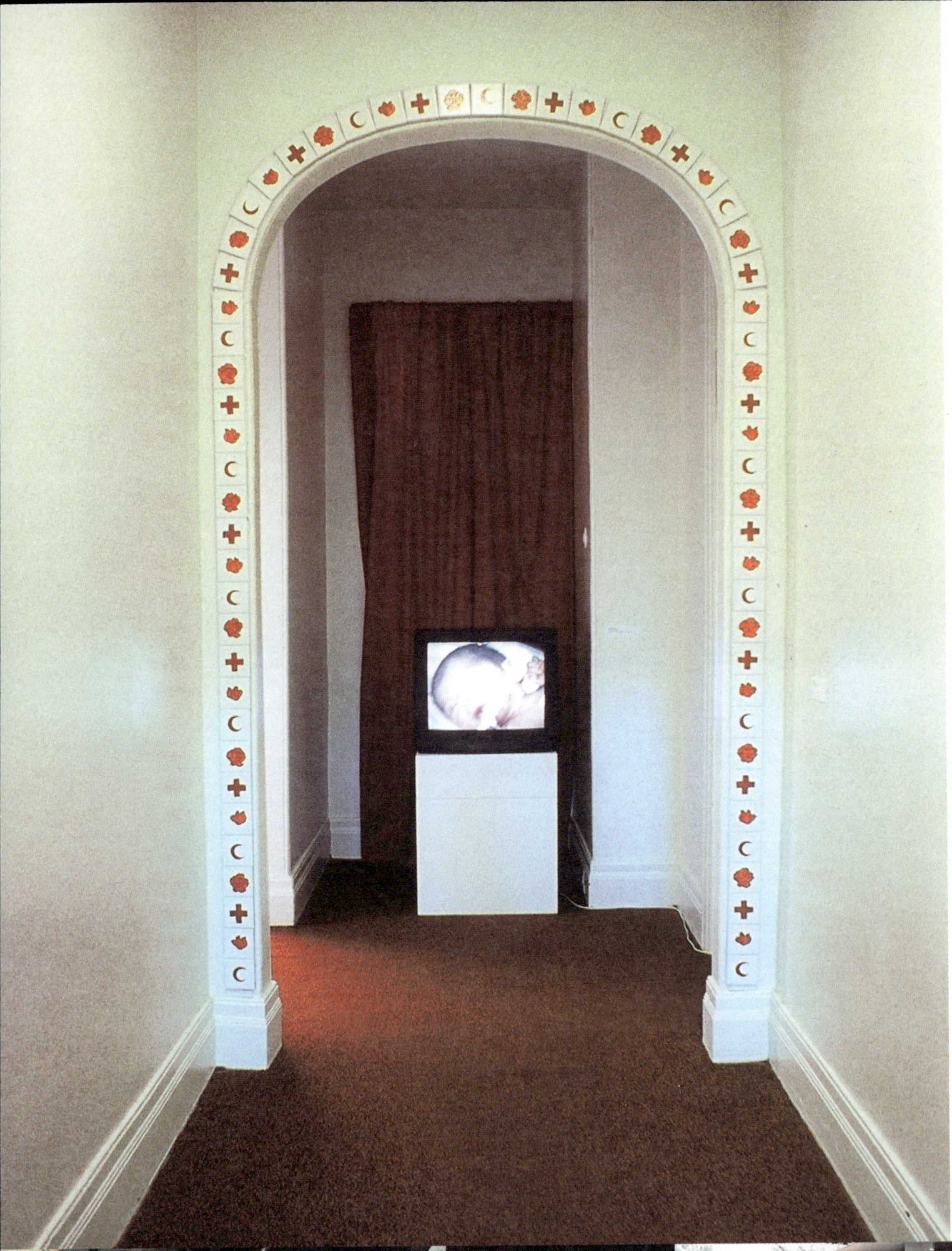

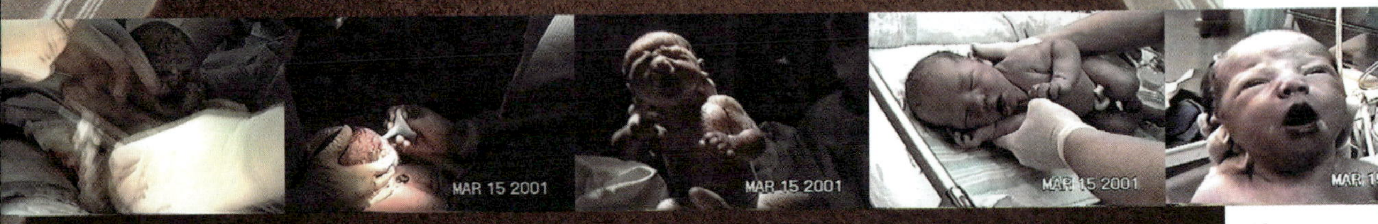
MAR 15 2001
MAR 15 2001
MAR 15 2001

JAMELIE HASSAN

Museum of Health Care at Kingston

FOR JAMELIE HASSAN, THE REALMS OF THE PERSONAL, poetic and cultural converge in artworks that sensitively respond to their architectural context. At the Museum of Health Care, she strategically interspersed ceramics, photographs, paintings, readymades and videos created over a thirty-year span throughout the museum's displays and exterior. Housed in a former nurses' residence completed in 1904, the Anne Baillie Building resonated deeply for the artist, recalling her own experience as a nurse's aide in Rome and Beirut. For MUSEOPATHY, Hassan brought forward portions of her history and archives and combined them with the museum's noteworthy heritage and plethora of medical and surgical instruments, laboratory equipment, medicines and patient care items. Her intervention centred upon four motifs — water, rose, crescent, infant — which dovetailed in their concern with care-giving and cross-cultural dialogue.

By titling her intervention *The Well*, Hassan contemplated the intimate association of water with healing. On the pedimented façade, she installed a circular photograph of waves lapping a rocky Lake Ontario shoreline. Inside, a twin image reappeared next to a bucket of water and rope, traditional implements for drawing water. Other well iconography included a gouache by the artist of a verdant oasis in Lebanon, and a reproduction of a nineteenth-century painting of Rebecca at the Well. The biblical parable of charity — giving a drink to a stranger — correlated with the ethos of nursing and women's role in the history of medicine as mothers, nurses, midwives and doctors. For Hassan, water functions as a polysemic element: it can denote the bounty of nature, provide rejuvenation, and serve as the medium of kindness.

Hassan included rose petals and emblems in several locations, a reference to the tradition of giving students of the School of Nursing a lavish bouquet of roses upon graduation. In the Middle East, roses hold multiple significance as a flavour in cuisine, an aroma associated with spirituality, and an ingredient in traditional

Jamelie Hassan, detail, *The Well* 2001
Video courtesy of Alice and John Williams

remedies. The most surreptitious of Hassan's rose elements was a bottle of fragrant extract placed in the museum's display of patent medicines and pharmaceuticals — thus infusing the "wonder drugs" of Western medical practice with the floral sensibility of Arabic cultures.

Hassan's crescent motif marks an historic connection between the museum and the Middle East. In 1915, the No. 5 Stationary Hospital of Queen's University Hospital (renamed Kingston General Hospital) opened in Cairo to attend to First World War casualties. This geographical link sparked Hassan to include her own watercolour views of Cairo and to explore the similarities between Eastern and Western health organizations. For Arabic countries, Red Crescent Societies parallel the mandate of their sister organization, the Red Cross, in alleviating suffering, supporting humanitarian activities and providing relief operations. A pair of miniature nurse dolls from the artist's collection, one with a cap emblazoned with a red crescent, the other with a red cross, symbolized the sibling status of the institutions, and a leaded glass window bearing a crescent moon, highlighted in red by the artist, designated the museum as an honourary Red Crescent site.

Bringing such knowledge of the East into Western consciousness, Hassan attached an enigmatic sign to the museum building. Displaying the Red Crescent, the word "infirmary" in French and Arabic, and an arrow pointing towards the KGH entrance, it served as a helpful beacon to potential Middle Eastern patients. Museum visitors could purchase medical kits from the Middle East modified by the artist — and embrace the cross-cultural implications of caring in the event of their own emergencies or mishaps.

Like Hassan's other leitmotifs, that of the infant recurred several times. Next to the museum's nineteenth-century wicker newborn scale, an infant figurine introduced by the artist rested on a bed of rose petals. On an adjacent wall hung a photograph of Hassan's son as a baby, swaddled in a birthing blanket. Such familial intimacy intensified in the museum's central hallway. A Tunisian-inspired arch composed of handpainted ceramic tiles (featuring roses, crescents and crosses) framed a monitor screening graphic footage of two caesarean births. Here visitors witnessed the excitement of the moment of birth experienced by family members and shared by medical personnel as they skilfully deployed surgical technology.

The Well was a complex multi-level intervention that suggested a process of becoming rather than a state of resolution. At once a personal archeology and serendipitous retrospective, the arrangements of medical objects, autobiographical artifacts and site-specific artworks reflected upon the intertwining of private and institutional histories and forged compelling links across cultural and geographical differences.

Infant image courtesy David Gordon

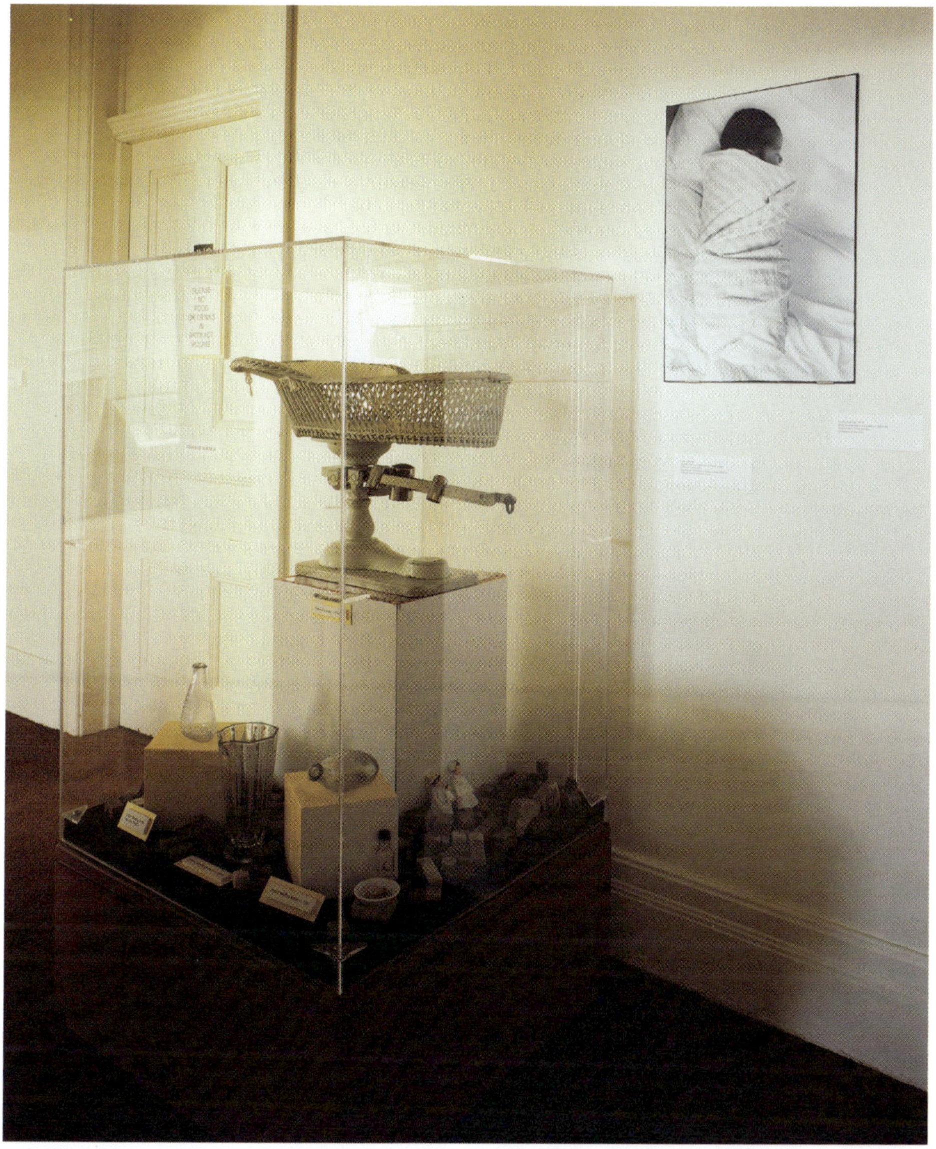

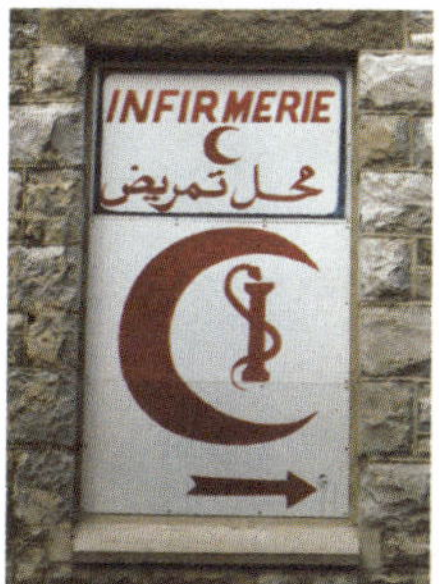
INFIRMERIE
محل تمريض

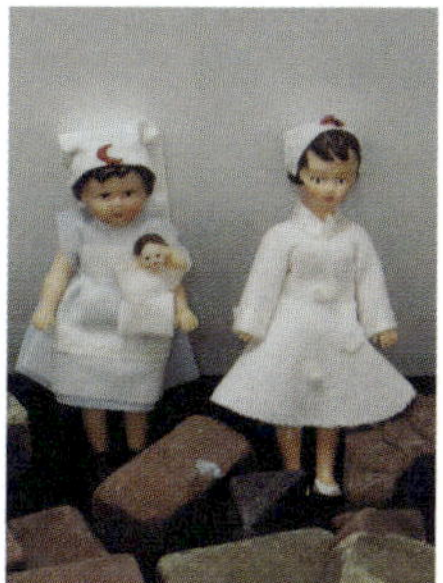

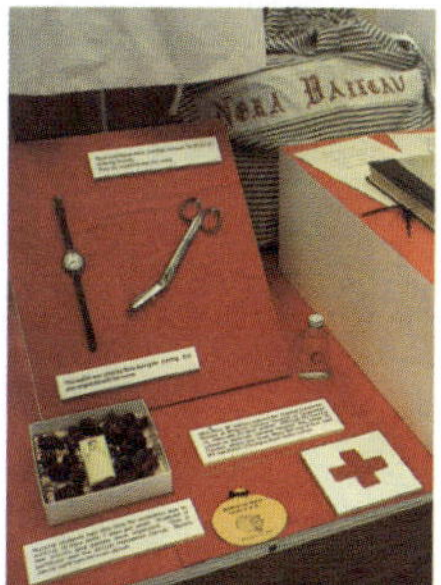

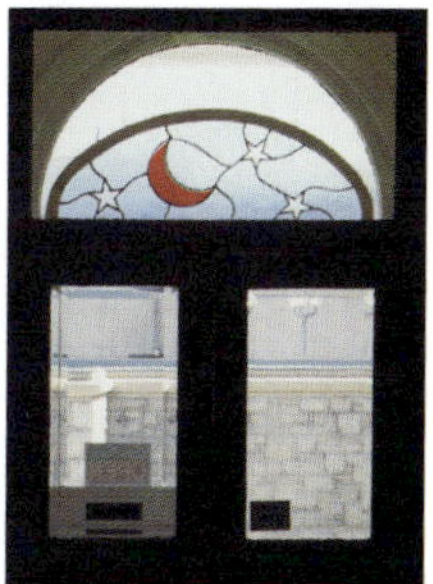

BARB HUNT

Royal Military College of Canada Museum

HOUSED IN A MARTELLO TOWER ON THE POINT at Fort Frederick, the Royal Military College of Canada Museum resides on the training grounds for the military officers of Canada's unified Forces. The location, where Lake Ontario and the Saint Lawrence River conjoin, is strategically and historically significant. Although never fired upon, the tower was built in the 1840s to counter the threat of war with the United States during the Oregon Crisis. After serving as a fortification and barracks, its rooms now exhibit RMC memorabilia, uniforms, orders and decorations of senior military officials, and a renowned collection of firearms and swords.

Barb Hunt's installation, *antipersonnel*, occupied the lower level, nestled into the arched chamber of a munitions magazine where gunpowder was formerly stored. A white, ziggurat-shaped shelf unit displayed 35 knitted life-sized replicas of anti-personnel mines accurately rendered in various shades of pink wool. What at first appeared to be cuddly playthings, miniature UFO's, tea cosies, potholders or erotic paraphernalia gradually materialized into representations of lethal devices. Painstakingly recreated from schematic diagrams, the fuzzy landmines were illuminated to make them glow and radiate. The use of fuchsia, rose and baby-pink stands in sharp contrast to the austere grey stonemasonry and the museum's dark furnishings. Decorative and military imperatives met incongruously, as the soft, pillowy objects impersonated explosive instruments of mutilation and death.

Displacing the metal and plastic constituents of conventional landmines with fibre implicitly linked knitting and war, as well as feminine and masculine military histories. By using softly textured, warm-hued wool, the faux landmines carried sensual associations and impelled the desire to touch them. This is an especially apt irony, since some landmines mimic the appearance of toys. The tactile curiosity of children cruelly results in lost limbs and lives. Both landmines and knitting bear a close, though inverse, association to the body — while one injures and causes

Barb Hunt, *antipersonnel* 1998-ongoing

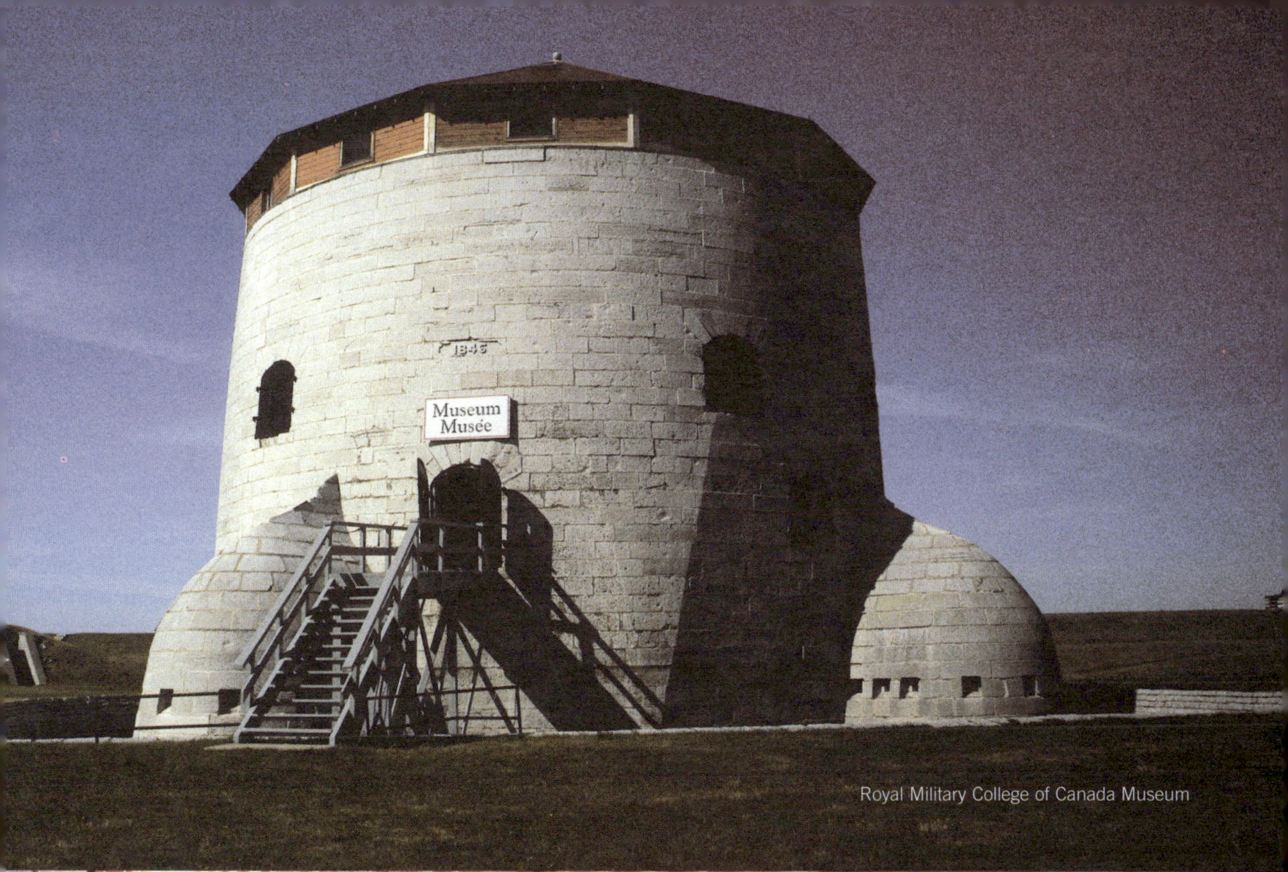

Royal Military College of Canada Museum

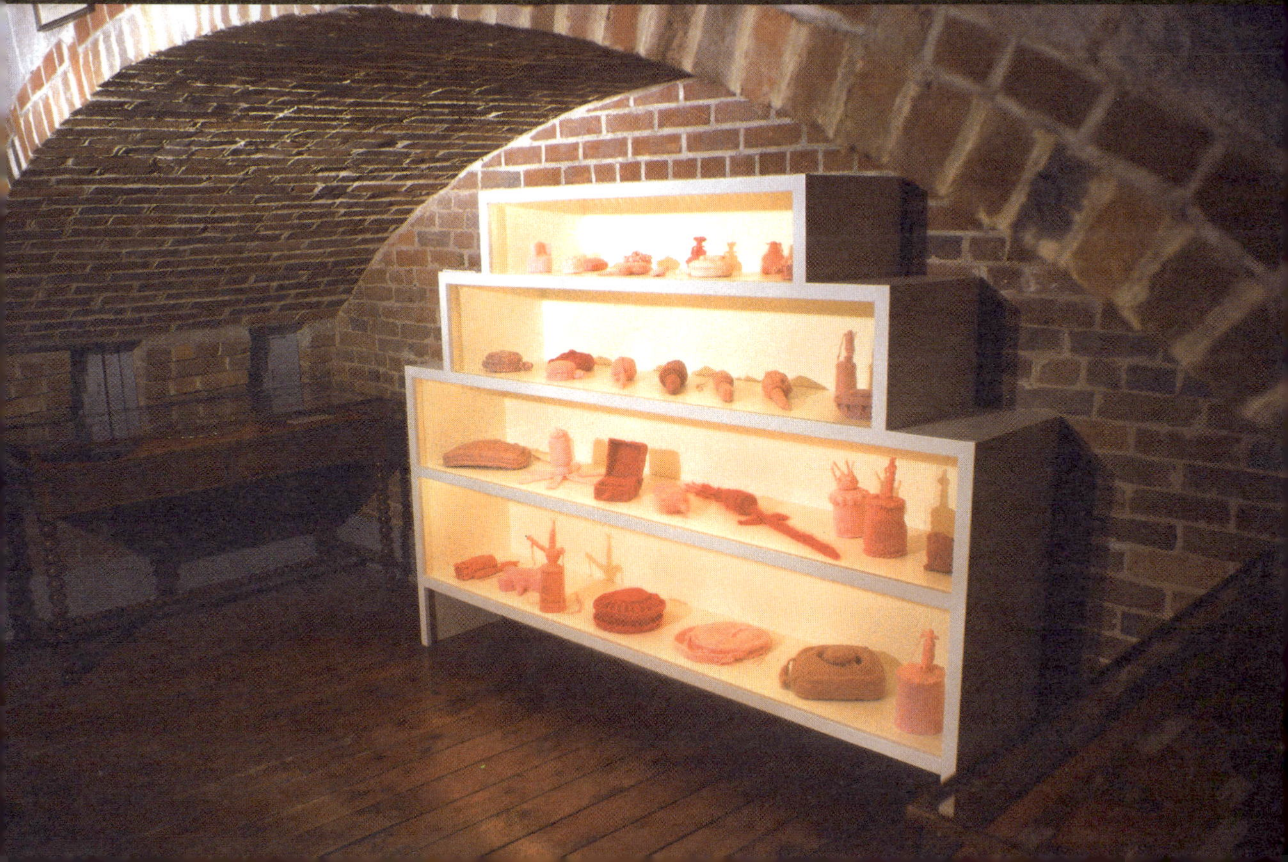

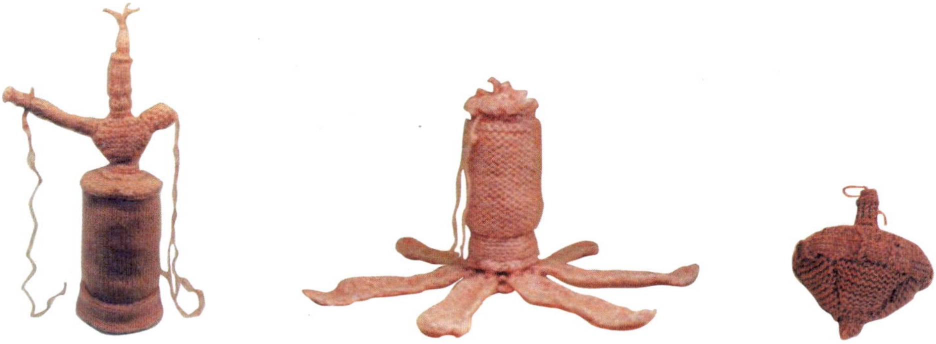

pain, the other provides succour and warmth. Knitting was at one time practised predominately by men (such as sailors and surgeons), but during the modern era one of the tasks expected of women was to knit bandages and socks for soldiers overseas. The practice of knitting thus functioned as a meditation on healing and protection, which Hunt recuperated as a metaphor for caring.

Hunt's landmines, created over a three-year period (and ongoing), reflect her longstanding interest in women's domestic textiles. Their production incorporated traditional knitting techniques she studied in Ireland, Newfoundland and France. These practices convey more than just material culture, for knitting has often functioned as the locus of political and personal discourses. During the French Revolution, for example, *tricoteuses* stitched the names and narratives of guillotine victims into wool garments. In Ireland and Newfoundland, knitting comprised not only a means of survival during times of agricultural and economic instability, but also a form of familial history that could be read into handmade clothing.

The artist's commitment to both activism and aesthetics signalled the ways in which craft and consciousness-raising have been important features in feminist praxis. On an aesthetic level, Hunt sought to explore the connective and experiential properties of fibre and its histories. On a pragmatic level, she aimed to demonstrate how small gestures, like stitches, can accumulate and eventually generate a web of

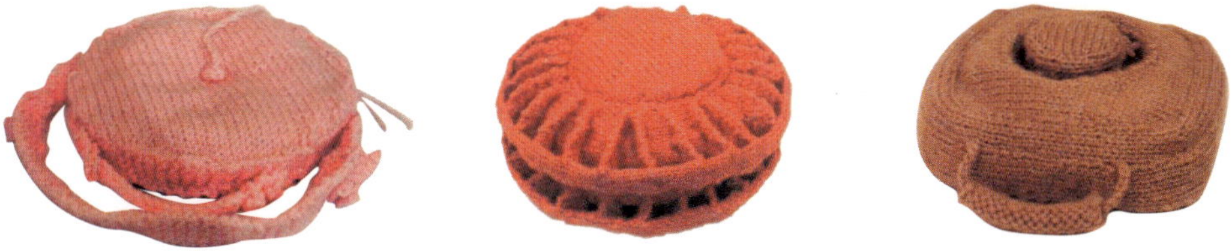

effective political resistance. Her stance against landmine use is commensurate with the official policy of Canada, which signed the anti-landmine treaty along with two-thirds of the world (the US so far has refused) and destroyed all its landmines. Alongside Hunt's reliquary of gossamery, harmless weapons, pamphlets provided information about the cause against landmines and directed readers to further resources and avenues for action.

antipersonnel transformed destructive weapons into subversive metaphors. Landmines are used by armies and guerrilla forces to control territory and intimidate civilian populations in war-torn areas. Simple, low-tech and cheap to install (more than 200 million are planted in the ground worldwide), they are a hundred times more expensive to remove than to produce, and pose a huge humanitarian problem in over sixty countries. In a museum commemorating Kingston's military past, these fluffy simulacra stood in for contemporary weaponry, foregrounding how the nature of warfare has changed from staged confrontations between professional soldiers in the nineteenth century to the militarization of the landscape and the targeting of entire populations in the twenty-first. By crafting objects which are normally mass-produced and carry such fatal intentions, Hunt not only brought a caring hand to the issue, but gestured to beholders to advance a campaign for peace.

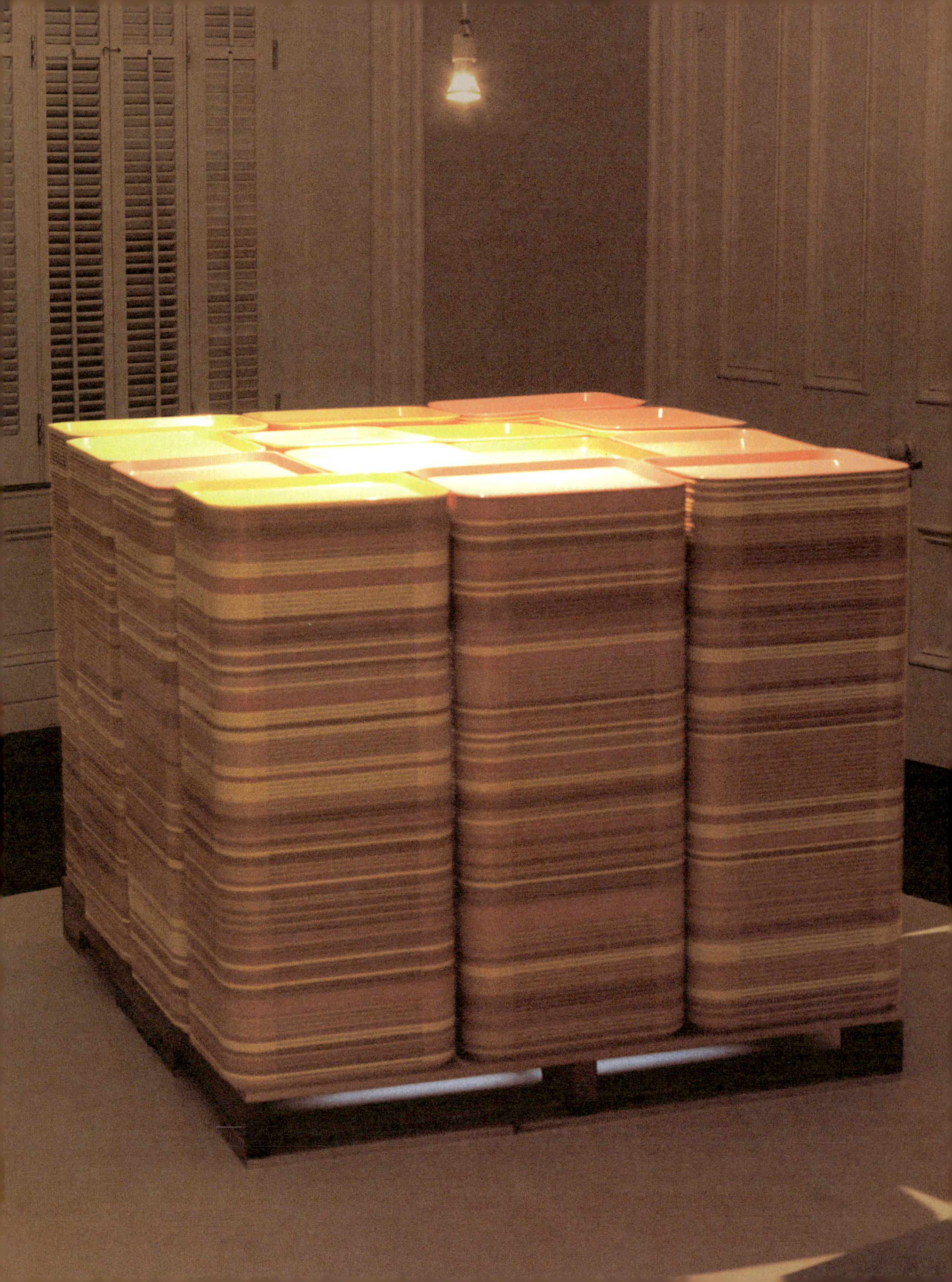

BRIAN JUNGEN

Correctional Service of Canada Museum

WORKING AT THE CROSSROADS OF ABORIGINAL and Western cultures, Brian Jungen transforms everyday, consumer objects into artifacts resonant with First Nations values. Gaining notoriety with sculptures that reconfigured Nike Air Jordan running shoes into forms reminiscent of West Coast ceremonial masks, and outdoor lawn furniture into the bleached skeleton of a whale, his works reference displays found in ethnographic and natural history museums.

Jungen's installation for MUSEOPATHY was inspired by the creativity of prisoners' bricolage exhibited at the Correctional Service of Canada Museum. The museum, housed in a Victorian limestone building that was built by inmates and originally served as the residence for Kingston Penitentiary's warden, contains a plethora of confiscated objects that attest to the stark conditions of prison life. The threat of violence is conveyed by numerous varieties of "shivs" and "shanks," hand-held concealable weapons imaginatively wrought from improbable materials such as toothbrushes, broken glass, pens, razors and broom handles. Displays of dummy heads patiently crafted from papier maché, barbershop clippings and mops compellingly illustrate the desire for escape that must be a major preoccupation during the monotonous hours of incarceration. Both types of prisoner-made paraphernalia evidence remarkable ingenuity in sensing the radical possibilities of ordinary objects; it is a working methodology with which Jungen felt an immediate kinship.

Isolated Depiction of the Passage of Time was the artist's response to one of the most infamous objects in the museum's collection — an escape pod fashioned from a hollowed-out stack of lunch trays clandestinely hoarded from the prison cafeteria. The object was built in 1980 by a prisoner from Millhaven Maximum Security Institution who knew that trays and dishes were sent for cleaning at Bath, a minimum security facility thought to be an easier launch for an escape. Gluing together scores of trays, carving out their interiors, and dieting to lose weight, he squeezed into the

Brian Jungen, *Isolated Depiction of the Passage of Time* 2001 stack's interior and successfully escaped Millhaven, though he could not elude authorities for long and was recaptured.

Jungen's sculpture likewise employed plastic lunch trays (nearly fifteen hundred) in what was at once an homage to the cleverness of the Millhaven inmate, and a wry appropriation of an icon of late-modernist sculpture and the signature form of minimal art. This cubic mass, in contrast to the formal and phenomenological gambits posed by Robert Morris or Donald Judd, reverberated with postmodern and political overtones. The first indicator of difference lay in its base, a delivery pallet painstakingly carved from western red cedar, a material intimately associated with Northwest Coast native mask-carving and totem poles. Secondly, the exuberant colours of the trays yielded little joy; lit by a single spotlight and situated in a darkened room, an ambiance of foreboding and anxiety prevailed. And thirdly, the colours and number of the trays were not arbitrary but politically poignant — they correlated to the number of aboriginal males incarcerated in Canadian penal institutions. Each tray represented an individual, and the five colours (orange, light pink, pink, mustard, yellow) corresponded to the sentences meted out (life, ten or more years, six to ten years, three to six years, and less than three years, respectively). When examined as a percentage of the general population, a disproportionate number of aboriginal men are imprisoned. The sculpture functioned like an imposing, three-dimensional bar graph, one that gave concrete, visible reality to an abstract collection of data and absent inmates.

The serving trays thus directly implied the notion of "serving time." Yet there was more than one understanding of time manifested in the installation: the legally

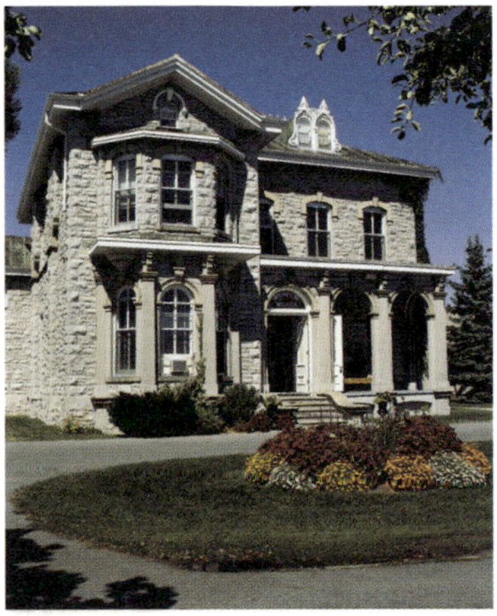

Correctional Service of Canada Museum

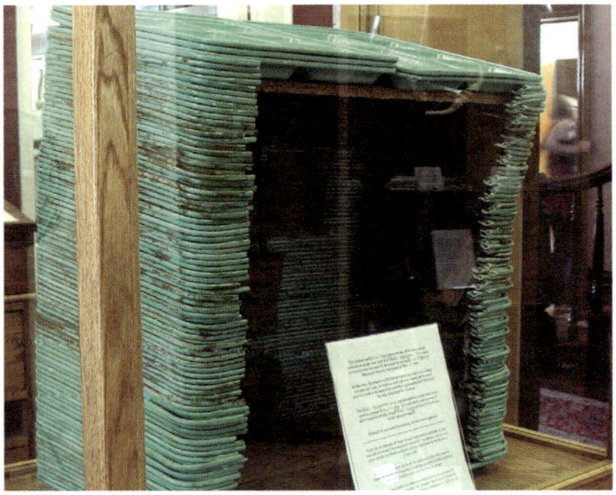

Inmate Escape Pod, 1980

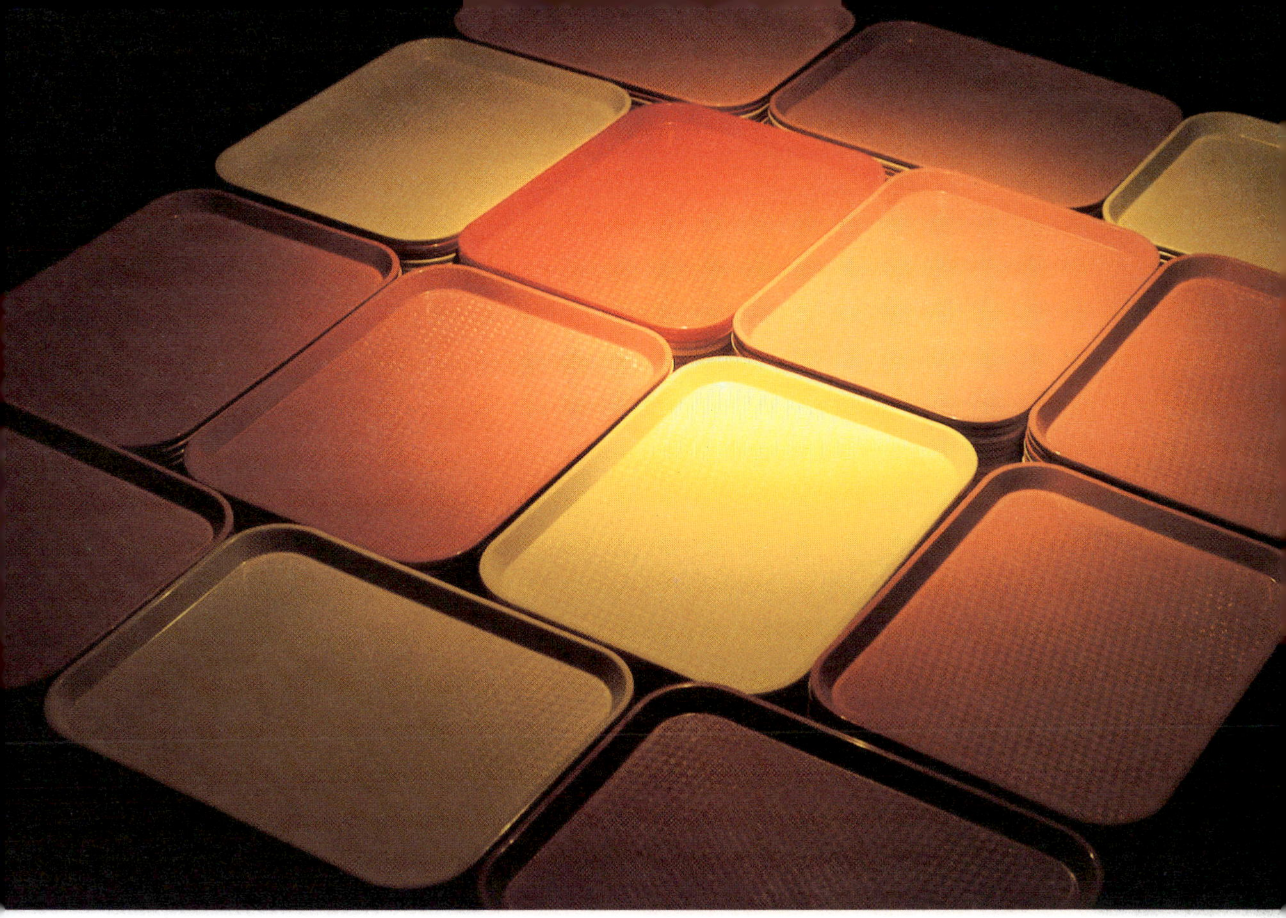

mandated degree of punishment (lengths of sentences) and the psychological experience of duration (one moment merging into the next). To evoke the latter, Jungen encased a television in the central cavity, a presence nearly imperceptible except for the faint blue glow visible between the slats of the pallet and the subtle buzz of dialogue and commercials. While voices could be heard and shows identified by their distinctive soundtracks, the actual dialogues between Oprah and her guests, commentators on CNN, and Vancouver newscasters could only be guessed at. Unbeknownst to viewers, the commentary emanating from the monitor related to the execution of Timothy McVeigh. For the artist, this was an uncanny coincidence — but one that nevertheless raised pertinent questions concerning criminality, punishment, media and national differences in penal policies. The television, residing within the trays much like the attempted escapee, animated the seemingly inert bulk — but only to convey the inertia and boredom of prison existence.

KOMAR AND MELAMID, with WILLIAM McCLELLAND

Grant Hall Tower, Queen's University

FROM THE BELL TOWER OF GRANT HALL at Queen's University, Komar and Melamid broadcasted *Call to Art* — a missionary salutation rendered in choral polyphony. The harmonic "call" rang out every half-hour like a thunderclap pervading the street and plaza adjacent to the Agnes Etherington Art Centre. Surprised passersby stopped in their tracks and raised their heads skyward to discern the origin of the sound. Reverberating throughout the campus landscape, these sonic bursts, though unexpected and mysterious, were at the same time sonorous and ecstatic.

Komar and Melamid collaborated with William McClelland who composed the calls and directed the twenty-person choir, the William Appling Singers of New York City. The lyrics written by Komar and Melamid and converted into music were utterly simple, the single word "art," which McClelland then expanded, layered, embellished and melodically complexified into sumptuous aural renditions of sublimity. These transcendent calls have been composed and recorded in more than six languages, and MUSEOPATHY marked *Call to Art*'s world premiere. Four English calls alternated throughout the day with each lasting between seven to fifteen seconds, transmuting an otherwise succinct word into a mellifluous, extended chorale.

Like muezzins summoning believers from their minarets or church bells announcing Christian liturgies, *Call to Art* echoed the "call to prayer" which exists in many religious faiths. Komar and Melamid drew upon a long history of sacred aspirations being channelled through aesthetic media, whether to motivate and educate worshippers, enhance the beauty of rituals and holy architectures, manifest the divine in provocative sensory presences, or provide the devout with a communal sense of identity. Also engaged were art's salvific and therapeutic powers — those

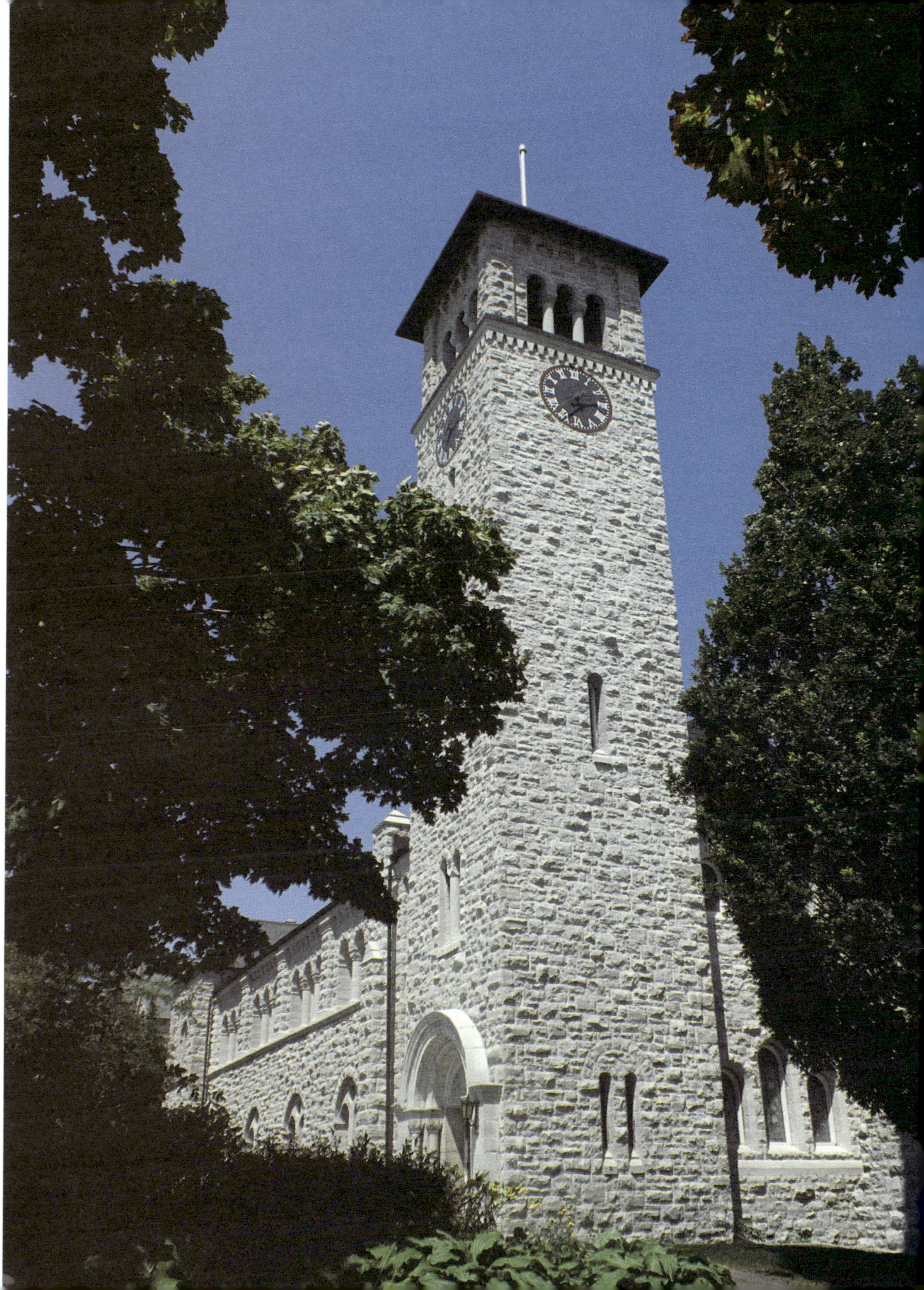

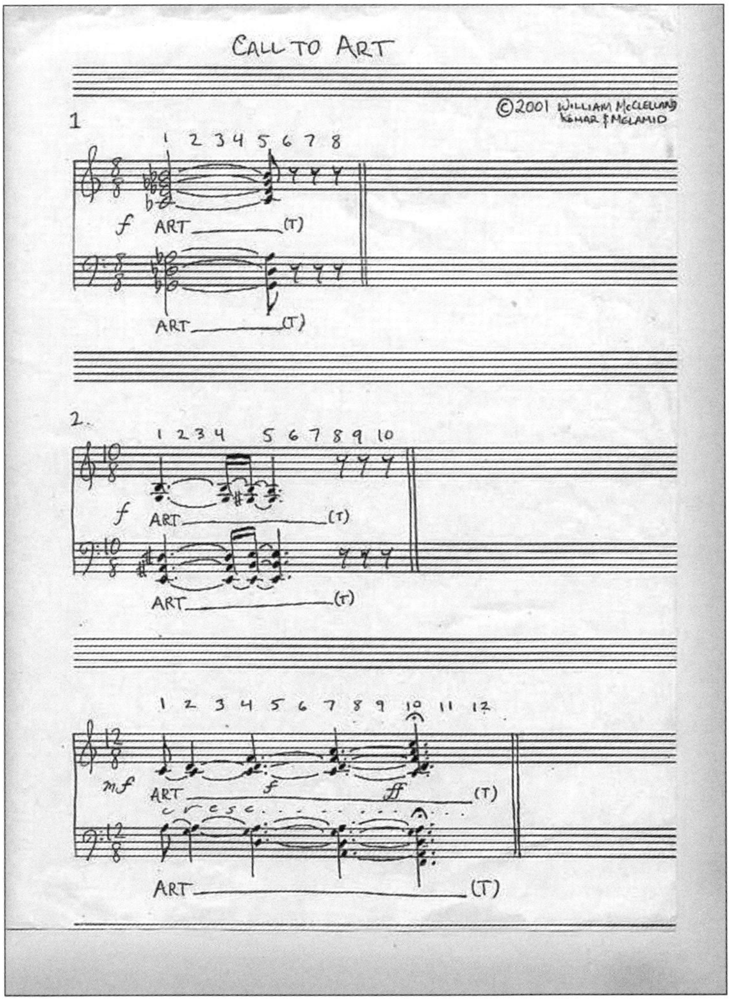

Komar and Melamid/William McClelland, score for *Call to Art* 2001

abilities to heal, inspire and transform cited by legends and historical accounts. Their urge to tap the spiritual energies of art was one that also aimed to avoid cooptation by religious institutions or adherence to a particular ecumenical position.

Irreverent reverence neatly sums up Komar and Melamid's working method. As in their series of paintings on the cult of Stalin, which satirized the leader's pretensions to glory while nostalgically affirming the paternal status of "Uncle Joe," the artists are at once deeply ironic and absolutely faithful to their subjects. *Call to Art* comprises one part of a larger project that parodically explores the parallels between art and forms of religious devotion. Plans are in the works to conduct missionary outreaches, undertake pilgrimages to sanctified art sites, set up a speaking tour delivering sermons and "preaching art," and build humble wayside chapels to famous popular artists, such as Van Gogh. "Art," they state, "is the true religion of the twentieth and twenty-first centuries," with museums as "the new houses of worship."

Call to Art did not idealize artists as godlike figures, but rather posited the museum as an arena of secular sanctity that can adopt the community function that once was the privileged domain of the church. It presented an invitation to invoke art and draw people into art's exhibition spaces in terms of an aesthetics based on connectivity and belonging. The intention was not to proselytize, but to recuperate the sociality of the museal realm as an *agora* or gathering space. At one point in their career, Komar and Melamid bought and sold souls (Warhol's included); now with *Call to Art* and the rest of their "religious" art they seek to collect and (scepticism aside) "save" them.

The artists traced the impetus of their work to the onset of Romanticism, when art filled the spiritual vacuum created by the Enlightenment's rational, anticlerical imperatives. In the intervening two hundred years, however, art has lost its ability to foster unmediated metaphysical experience because of bureaucratization, commodification and the drive for institutional power. The artists claim that art professionals now constitute a new clergy, acting as gatekeepers, deciding what is worthy or not, and obscuring the public's access to aesthetic experience. That the building of museums nowadays gains more prominence than the works housed within them testifies to the inversion of values Komar and Melamid decry. The answer — they claim sincerely with tongues in cheek — is to open up the church of art, put people in close proximity to great works, and democratize the artistic experience. It was difficult to gauge whether Komar and Melamid, once known as arch postmodernists, were authentic believers in their own discourse, but whatever their spiritual commitments, the ethereal melodies of *Call to Art* certainly extended this artwork beyond purely ironic intentions.

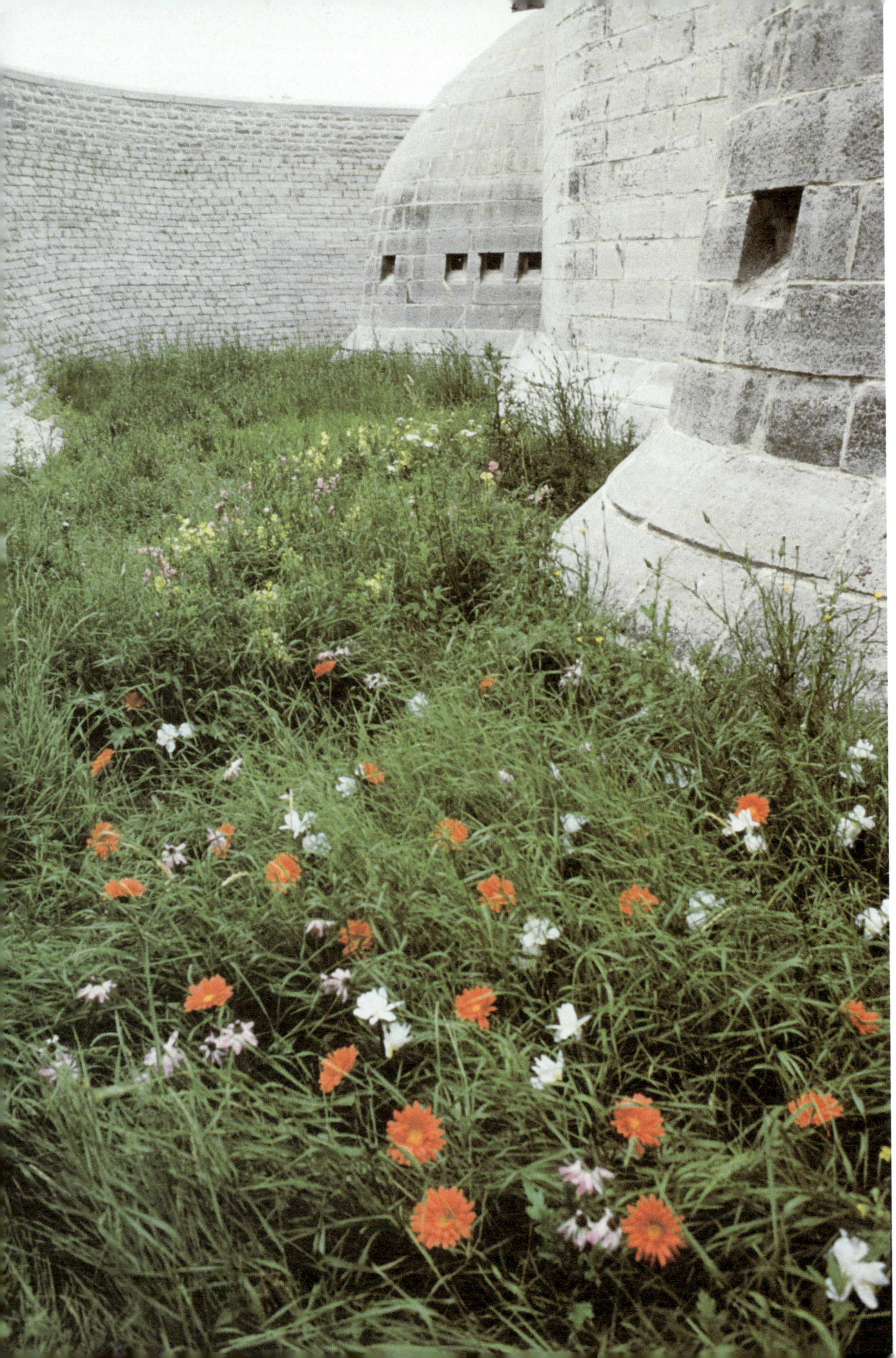

ANNE RAMSDEN

Murney Tower National Historic Site

"My name is Alice Richie although I prefer to call myself Violet." So began the introspections of a nineteenth-century soldier's wife, the creation of Anne Ramsden's historical research and creative license. Violet's musings about the hardships of her situation and hopes for a new life beyond this military outpost were set during the period when the Murney Tower housed the soldiers and families of the Royal Canadian Rifle Regiment (1848–1890). Her comments about winter's isolation, the difficulty in finding employment, and the joys of relaxing by the lake brought forward the little-known domestic dimension of this imposing fortification.

Ramsden's artworks often contemplate museums as places where artifacts construct historical worldviews. Her intervention here, *Garden*, installed discreetly throughout the building and grounds, drew attention to the encounter between the traditionally separate domains of feminine and masculine activities, the duties of war and the nurturing of families. This unexpected confluence is broached briefly in one of the site's permanent displays: a nineteenth-century photograph depicting the tower adorned by curtains and flowerpots. Ramsden's multi-part installation de-emphasized the grand narratives of martial engagement and subtly magnified women's sensibilities and subjective experience.

Ramsden mobilized a characteristically nineteenth-century feminine decorative tradition — the floral — to intervene into the tower's military history. On the main floor, which served as the Regiment's living quarters, the artist arranged in a vitrine eighteen antique tea cup saucers, each strewn with flower seeds. The text of Violet's ruminations rested in the space framed by the saucers, mounted and rendered in a typeface commensurate with surrounding interpretive panels. Violet's use of the first-person singular, however, markedly contradicted the third-person museological narratives provided elsewhere. The "I" telling the story made present a woman's voice and specific personality within the conventions of neutral and

Anne Ramsden, detail, *Garden* 2001

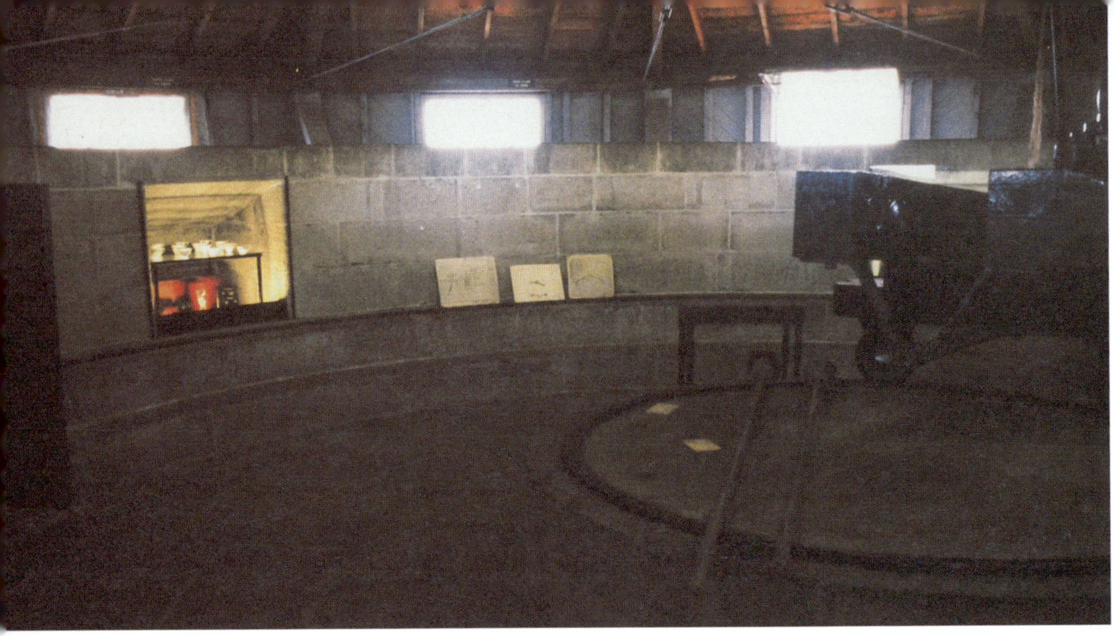

View of gun platform, *Garden* 2001

objective discourse. Violet's text — which might be misconstrued as "true" history — troubled expectations of authenticity and alerted readers to the various degrees of fabrication necessary to the presentation of history.

The companion cups to the saucers were located on the top floor, the gun platform. Set in a niche normally housing cannonballs, their elegant decoration contrasted sharply with the tower's dense, grey masonry, immense wooden beams and powerful Bloomfield cannons. The dramatic difference in material and sensorial attributes reflected antithetical realities. Whereas the flowered porcelain was fragile and designed to be held by genteel hands in refined social events, the mighty guns were lethal and only operable by teams of soldiers, probably under siege. On yet another level, the incongruous juxtaposition was perfectly lucid: women (their purity, beauty, safety) have often served as the justification for war, and the delicacy of tea rituals emblematized the civilized ideals and way of life militaries seek to defend.

In Violet's pensive text, she fantasized about a garden bursting with colourful blooms and enchanting fragrances. Her reverie was realized in the ditch encircling the tower — a forbidding zone of slanted stone embankments, designed to repel enemy intruders — where Ramsden "planted" a garden of flowers in carpetbedding style. Like so much domestic labour, a garden involves patience and humble tending — a counterdiscourse of cultivation and care to the military's rationale of defence. The flowers recalled, alternately, mourning rites and remembrance celebrations as well as antiwar protests and the "flower power" of the 1960s. By virtue of the

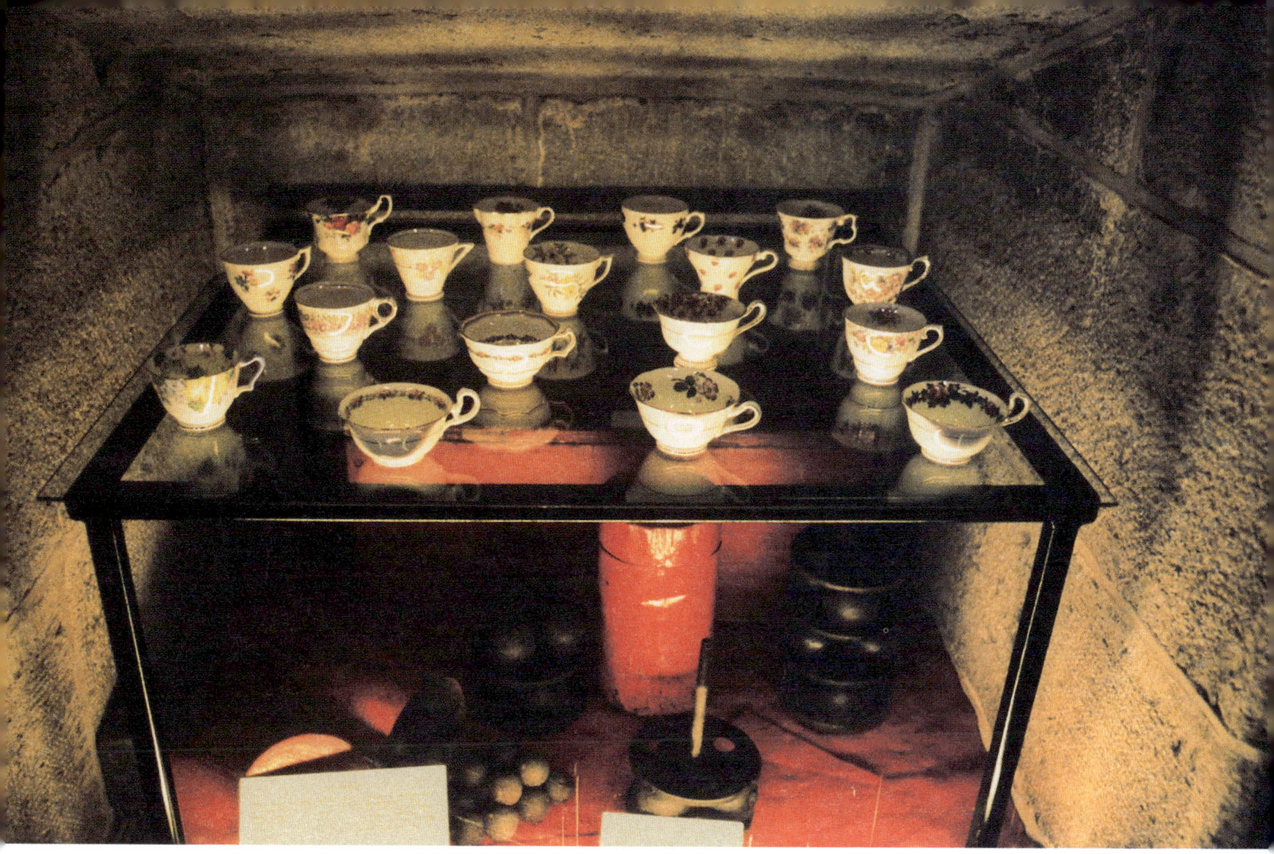

blossoms' position around a museum, one recognized that a garden is implicitly a "collection" — of plant species. To Canadians of British heritage, importing flower seeds to recreate the flora of the homeland was a common passion and a significant instance of how colonialism thrived on the more oblique level of biology, agriculture and domestic aesthetics.

Ramsden's flowers, in contrast to the intermixed grasses and weeds, were scentless, resisted drawing bees, never wilted, shed no petals. The reason was that the garden consisted of silken fakes. The unnaturally persistent blooms, extra-exuberant colours and fanciful shapes of this horticultural fantasy perfectly embodied the oneiric qualities of Violet's yearnings. Such an illusive combination of the factual and fictional infiltrated every aspect of Ramsden's intervention and served as its generative logic. *Garden* framed the site as a museological artifact reverberating with real and virtual histories. That the name of Ramsden's persona was taken from a trunk displayed in the museum underscored the practice of history itself as an enterprise that blends real evidence and imaginative insight.

MITCH ROBERTSON

International Ice Hockey Federation Museum

CELEBRITY, FAME AND FANDOM ARE PROMINENT and inescapable features of contemporary culture. For Mitch Robertson's intervention at the International Ice Hockey Federation Museum, these phenomena provided the essential link between the nominally opposed cultures of art and sport. The two-storey museum of green cinderblock walls and polished concrete floors, sited adjacent to a community arena and sports complex, became a context for a studied response to the culture of commemoration. Shuffling his works among the vitrines of Canadian and international hockey relics, photographs, jerseys, trading cards, banners and souvenirs, the artist brought into relationship the covert connections between hockey and art — as realms that share dynamics of struggle and competition, tribute and influence, reverence and achievement, popularity and renown.

Sport serves as a central defining element in many individuals' lives, whether it is considered to be diverting entertainment, professional spectacle or contests with elevated (some would claim metaphysical) dimensions. Robertson's interventions addressed many aspects of the sport-art continuum, and his works were placed throughout the space utilizing all of the available exhibition rhetorics, from the merchandising cabinets at the front desk to the video screening room in the rear. As visitors checked in with the attendant at the museum shop, they first saw examples of the artist's multiples: a pyramidal display of *World's Greatest* coffee mugs and shelves full of *Famous*™ *Artstar* cards. Here art, sport and collectibles self-consciously converged as notions of greatness and fame were available in convenient, affordable packages.

The first floor contained wallworks interspersed among hockey posters. *People I Know* consisted of hockey team photographs from the artist's youth. Only players whom Robertson now recognizes peer out at the viewer. Those whose names can't be recalled are obliterated with silver leaf, leaving shimmering but forlorn silhouettes —

Mitch Robertson, installation view and detail, *World's Largest Ball of Hockey Tape* 2001

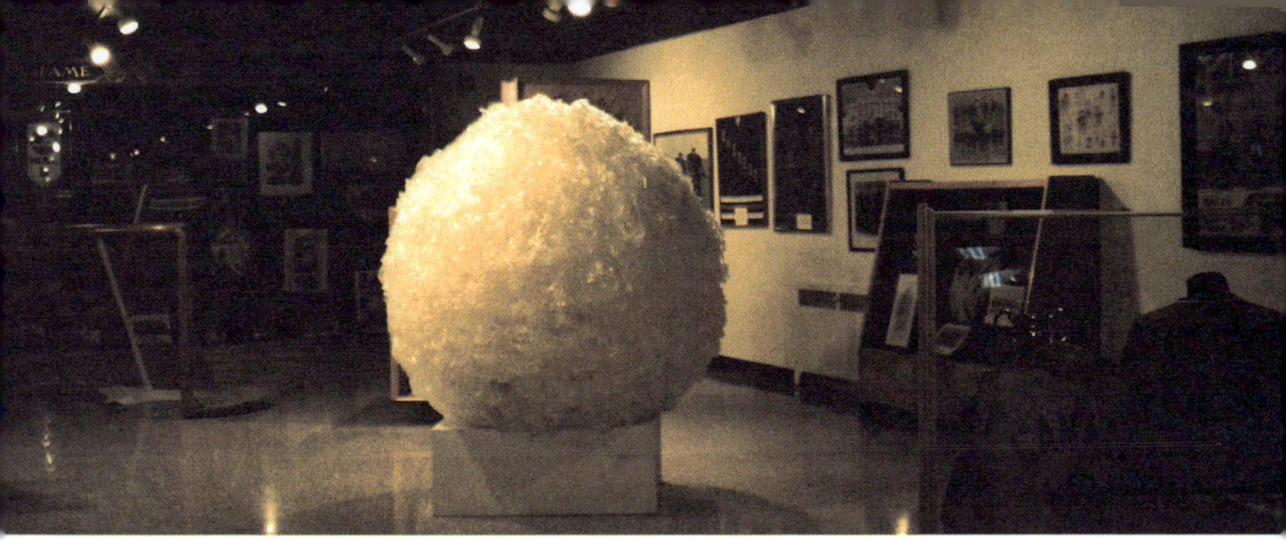

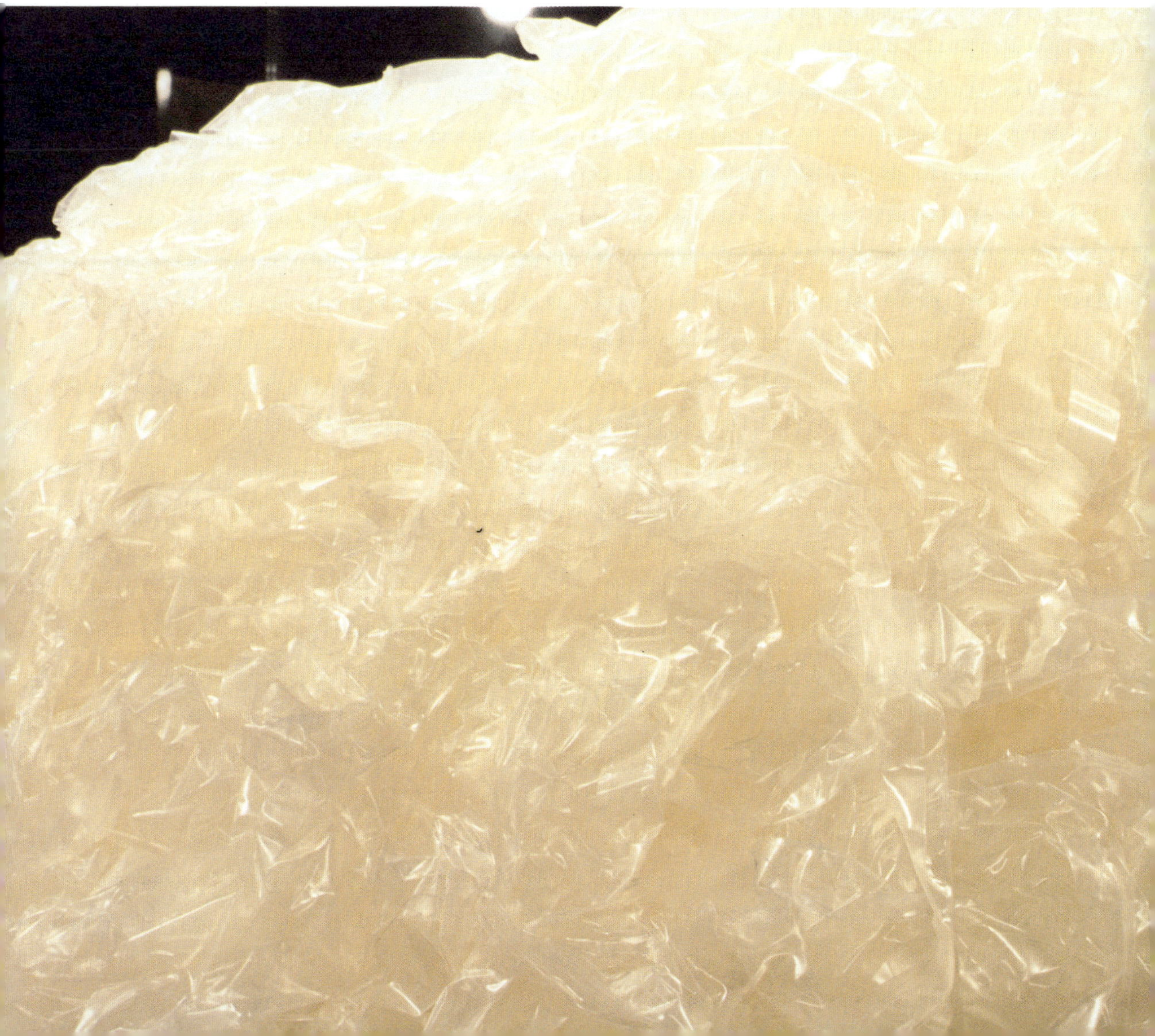

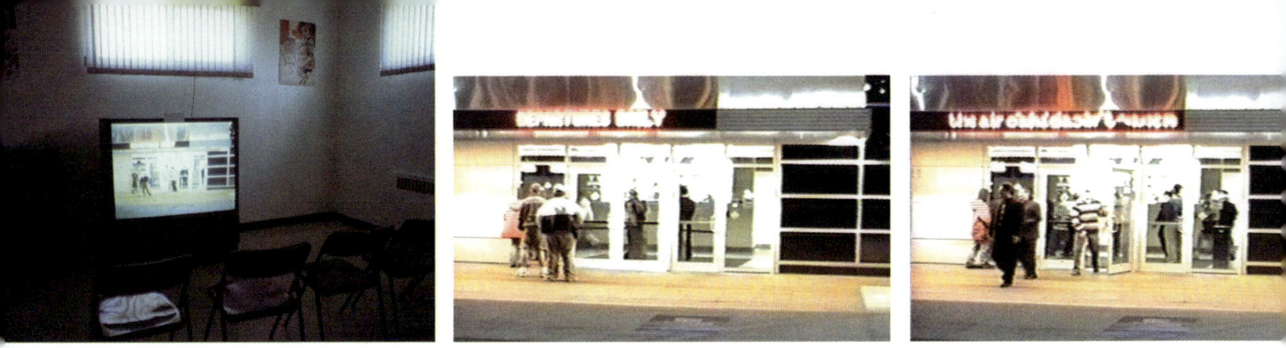

Mitch Robertson, installation view and stills, *Crowd Scene* 2001

a memorial to forgetfulness. A map entitled *Places I Have Been (Birth to Present)* referenced the artist's travels. Contrary to a similar one on display in the museum, which featured flags on numerous sites around the world, Robertson's betrayed a self-effacing and humorous effect, since his excursions thus far have been comparatively modest. Another series, *Lucky Numbers*, inscribed retired jersey numbers from each NHL team onto keno game cards, commenting on the gamble and risk inherent to hockey and its chances for reaping financial rewards or glory.

The hockey museum enshrines a Hall of Fame featuring hundreds of oak-framed photos of Canadian players such as Gordie Howe. In a room beside these hockey greats, Robertson presented the inverse — the numerous, anonymous fans whose appreciation spurred and followed these players' exploits. *Crowd Scene* focused on a set of doors at Toronto's Air Canada Centre and in a continuous 48-minute shot showed the exiting throng after a Maple Leafs game. At first a few people leave before game's end, then a horde gushes forth, ultimately dwindling to a few stragglers. The elementary but compelling kinaesthetic dynamics captured here recalled the very origins of cinema, such as the Lumière brothers' *Workers Leaving the Lumière Factory* (1895), but also evoked the fixed camera view and ambient anxiety (given hockey fans' unpredictable energy) of security surveillance video.

In the stairwell leading to the second floor, Robertson hung fifteen felt banners in the style of those found in arena rafters. Dedicated to artists considered influential to his own practice, these banners offered a name, birth year and colours derived from each artist's national flag. Their chronological order (ranging from Garry Neill Kennedy, 1935, to Alex Morrison, 1971) and elevated positioning suggested a ritualistic form of veneration as this personalized spiral of fame paid homage to artistic heroism and standards of accomplishment that Robertson admittedly both admires and seeks to exceed.

Given a museum context replete with competition and fame, Robertson audaciously arranged to set a world record. *World's Largest Ball of Hockey Tape* was inspired by the many hockey players who make balls out of the clear, honey-tinted

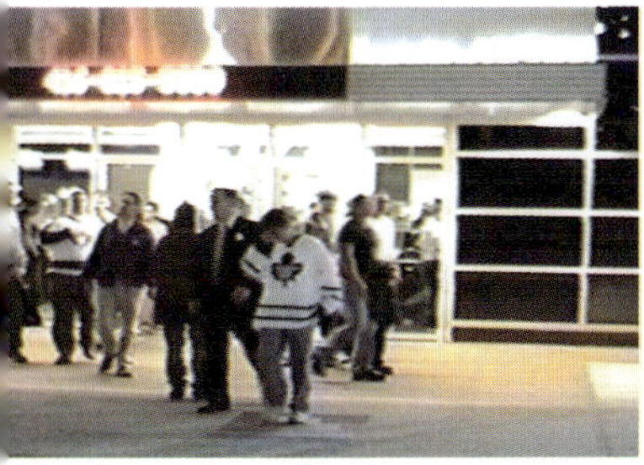
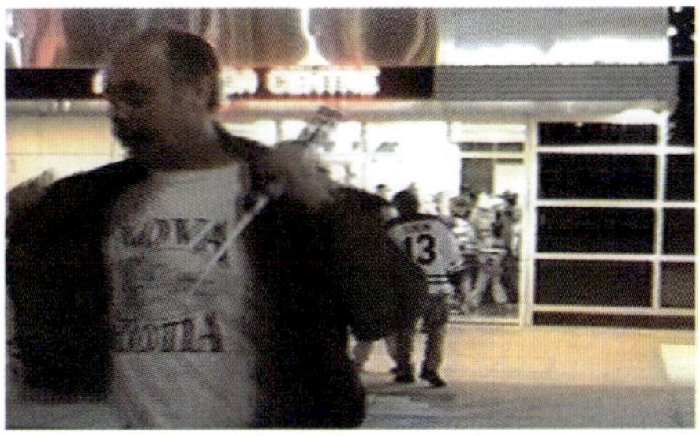
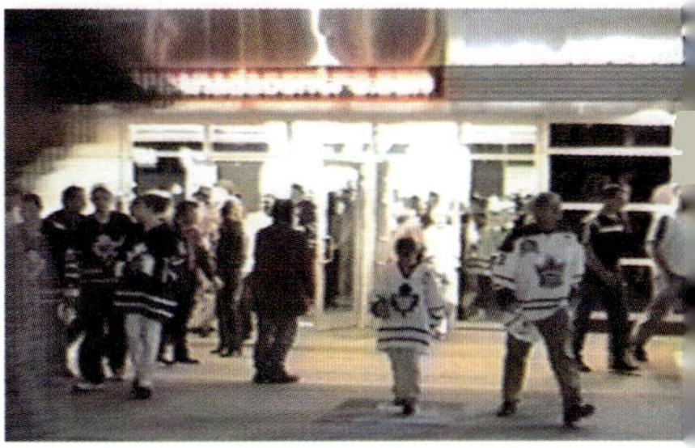

tape used to secure their socks. Robertson's effort involved the wrapping of 36 kilometres of tape into a looming, six-foot diameter ball. At MUSEOPATHY's launch it comprised a perfect, luminescent orb. But over the humid summer it shrank and settled, accumulating the patina of curious hands. While at once a minimalist reference to hockey and a testimony to the absurd desire for notoriety, it evolved into a surprisingly popular touristic marker and snapshot backdrop. Even though any sized ball would have won the title (there is currently no such category in the Guinness record books), Robertson's grandiose gesture, however strategic and playful, garnered the very sense of aura that great feats command.

Mitch Robertson, installation view, *My Hall of Fame* 2001

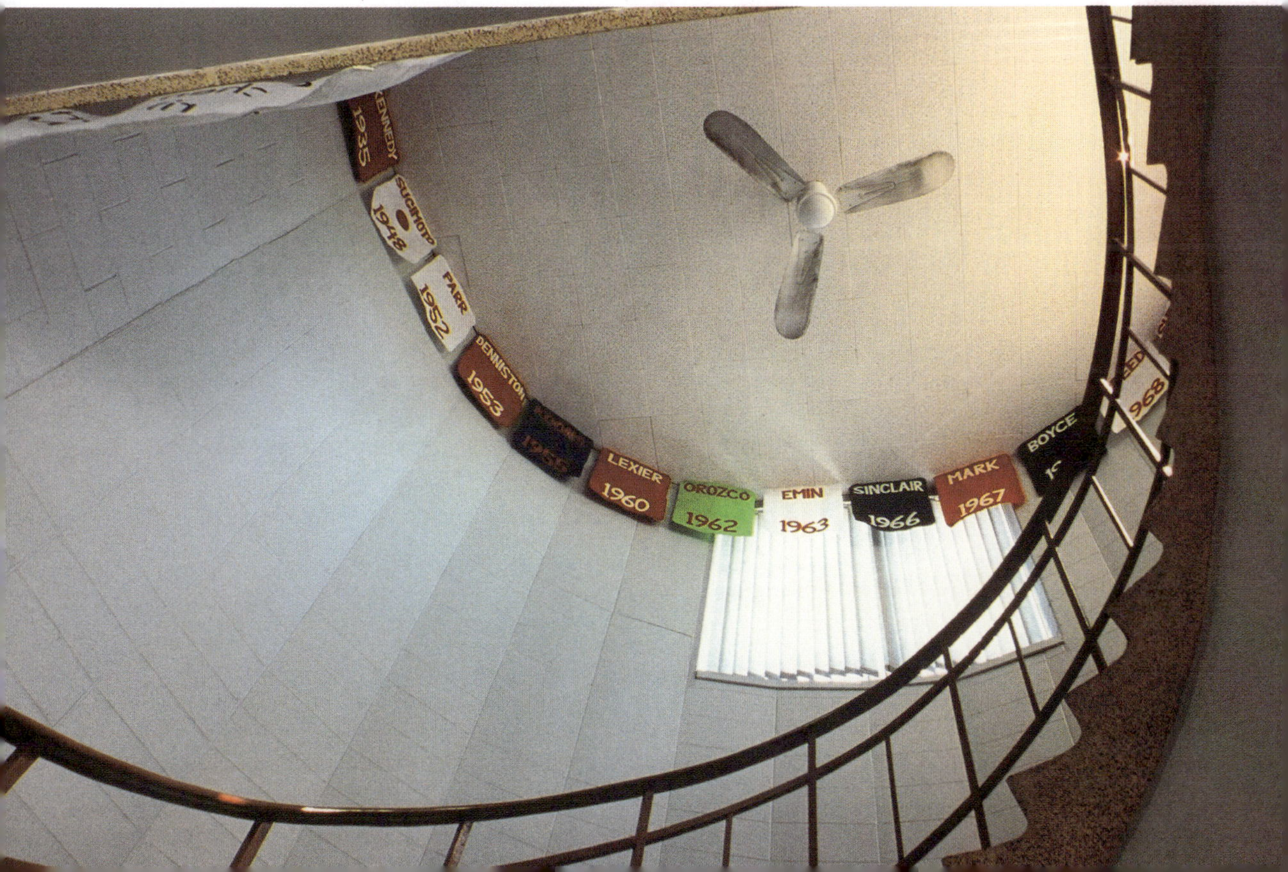

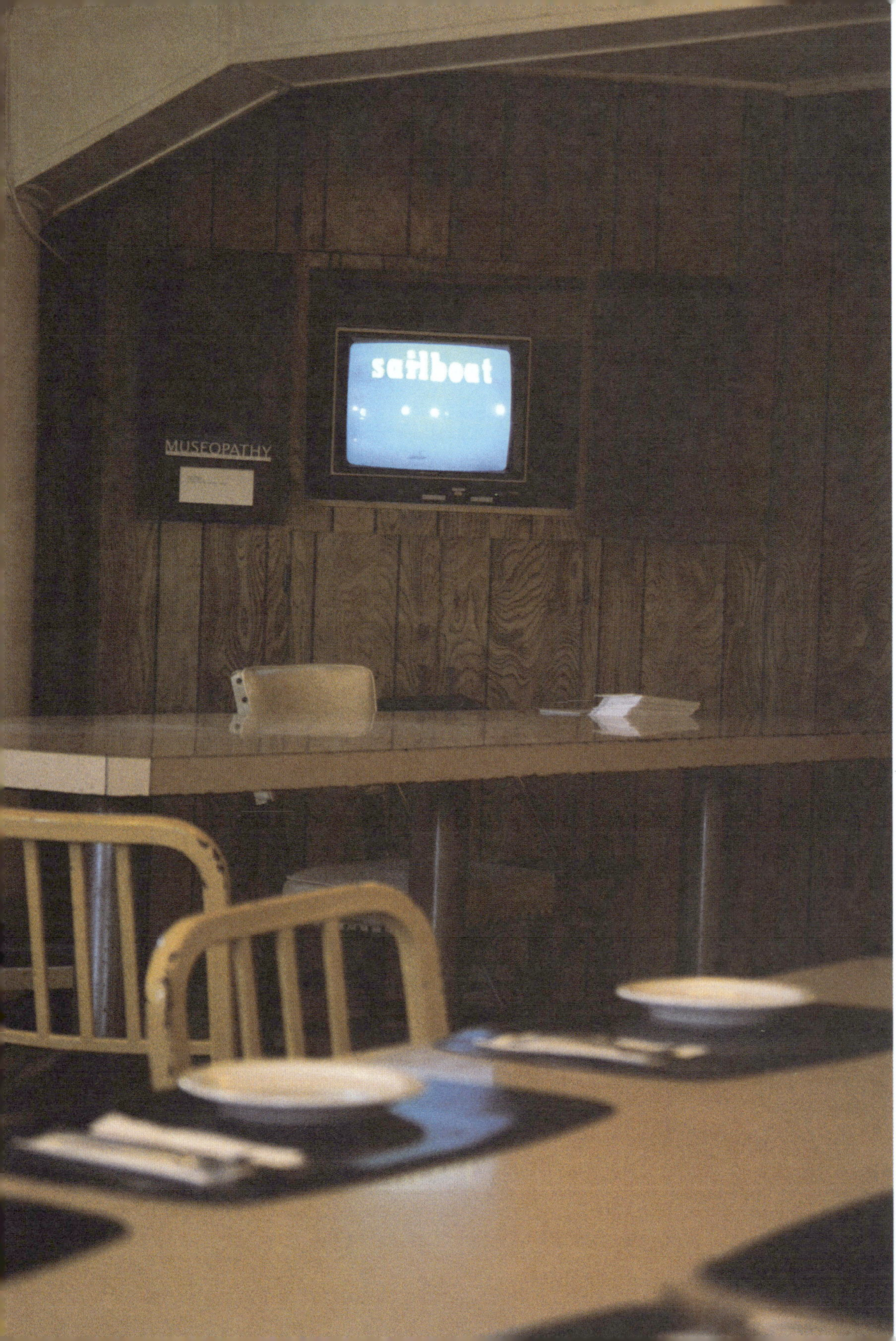
sailboat
MUSEOPATHY

JOYCE WIELAND

Museum Ship ALEXANDER HENRY

THE SCREENING OF JOYCE WIELAND'S FILM *Sailboat* occurred in a germane though unusual location — the mess hall of the Museum Ship *Alexander Henry*. Harboured within a television niche amidst a room full of tables, chairs, meal settings and portholes, a continuous video loop beamed the image of a sailboat on a windswept lake, buffeted by whitecaps. The enigmatic scene both appealed to and disturbed expectations of ship visitors after having negotiated through labyrinthine passages, massive machinery and tight quarters.

This experimental film challenged the perception of time through the depiction of a sailboat's progress and eventual disappearance into a monochromatic blue horizon. In multiple cuts, a sailboat entered the frame from the left, bobbed across the water, then exited on the right. The film adopted an oceanic rhythm, as each scene followed the other in a series of waves. To a soundtrack of hypnotic static, the sequence of nearly identical images proceeded in a trancelike fashion, seemingly without development or denouement. The regularity of the boat's movements conflicted with the stillness of the camera, generating a tension in the otherwise meditative experience. The only unexpected intrusion occurred when a boy leapt into the frame and down the beach to the water, giving viewers the decisive clue that the film was not a duplication of the same shot spliced one after the other, but a real-time (though extremely minimalist) narrative.

To create the film, Wieland apparently positioned the camera, took a shot, then picked up the gear, ran down the beach, and resituated the camera so that the sailboat would reenter the frame on the left, repeating the procedure a dozen or so times. At first the boat was near the shore, but after four cinematic minutes it receded into the blurry distance where sky, vessel and water merge indistinguishably. This aesthetic strategy finds its origins in Wieland's keen interest in structuralist and process-oriented filmmaking. Typical of her genre, the experience of space was

Joyce Wieland, installation view, *Sailboat* 1967

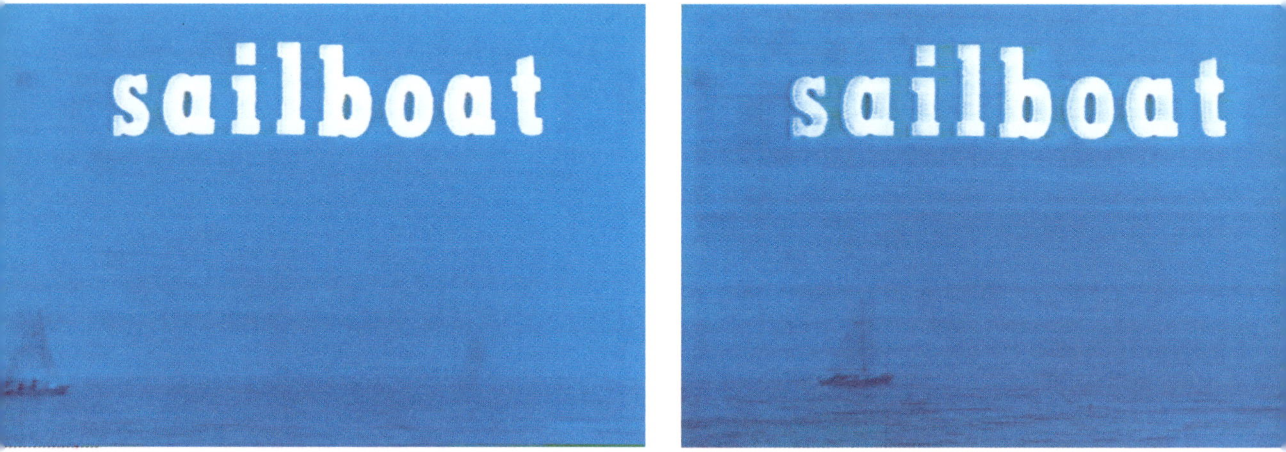

Joyce Wieland, film stills, *Sailboat* 1967

flattened, underscored by the word "sailboat" stamped over the film in block letters. The noun became a visual marker with as much or greater presence than the image of the sailboat itself, inverting the conventional subordination of the title to its referent.

Joyce Wieland (1931–1998) influenced both the development of feminist art aesthetics and the Canadian discourse on nationalism, ecology and gender. Her oeuvre encompassed a variety of media, ranging from assemblage and textiles to painting and film. *Sailboat*, produced while the artist was living in New York City, reflected her fascination with American culture and its preoccupation with grotesqueness and tragedy. Affected by JFK's assassination and Andy Warhol's disaster series, Wieland created a series of catastrophic ship paintings, including *Sinking Liner* (1963) and *Sailboat Sinking* (1965). These paintings were "filmic" in the sense that they incorporated sequences of images arranged like celluloid strips or film stills, prefiguring the actual cinematic resolution in *Sailboat*. As the film's eponymous craft voyaged away from shore, there was a hint of foreboding and unease; although less direct than her catastrophe paintings, a hint of the ominous permeated the action as the boat diminished from view and faded into nothingness.

The context of *Sailboat*'s screening, the *Alexander Henry*, contrasted with its subject of leisure boating and the femininely coded activity of beachside vacationing with children. During its 25 years of service it carried a crew of 34 men as it performed icebreaking duties and tended to the navigational aids of the Great Lakes. Named after a nineteenth-century fur trader and explorer who forged routes through

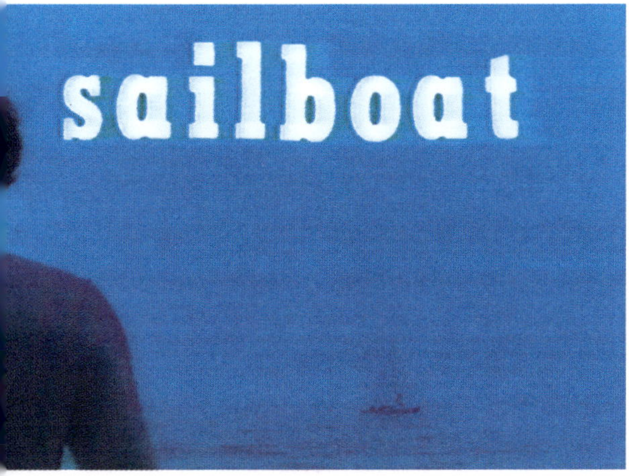

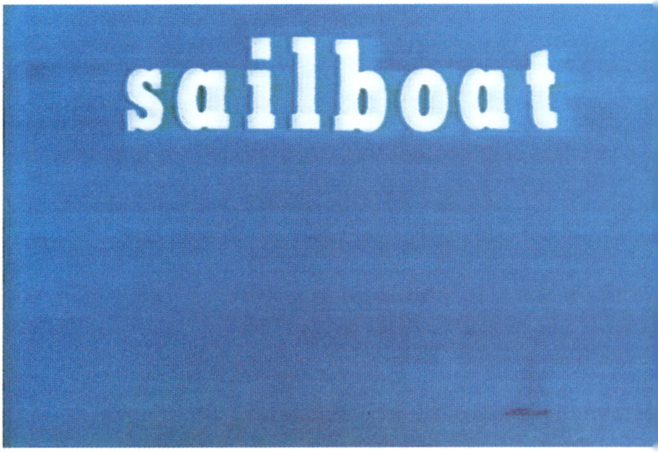

what was to become one of the world's major shipping lanes, the ship exemplified a distinctly masculinist culture of mechanical power, functionality and no-frills engineering. With the placement of Wieland's film on board, the Coast Guard encountered the avant-garde. A vessel ensuring marine safety and rescue became the *mise-en-scène* for an artist's observation of potential catastrophe. And if the minimalism of the film struck ship visitors as repetitive, it was perhaps a reminder that life aboard ship was not always dramatic or heroic, but one in which routine and habit were the basis of seaworthiness.

MEL ZIEGLER

Bellevue House National Historic Site

INTO THE TRANQUILLITY OF NINETEENTH-CENTURY period rooms, Mel Ziegler introduced contemporary and Victorian-style objects purchased from mail-order and electronic catalogues. Blending a concern for issues surrounding the merchandising and authenticating of artifacts, the current zeitgeist of historical ambiance in home decor trends, and the permeability of US/Canadian cultural relations, Ziegler's intervention positioned the museum as a nexus in the complex cultural network of taste and evaluation. The collecting activity of museums exists in continuity with more general practices of acquisition and display, and the artist animated one of Canada's national landmarks as a stage for raising questions about history, tourism and the function of the museum.

Mail Order Authenticity involved placing approximately fifty recent purchases by the artist into Bellevue House's time-stilled pre-Confederation interiors. With the exception of a few striking anachronisms, the new objects integrated seamlessly with regular museum artifacts. No didactic material was posted; the onus was on visitors to engage with a playful discovery of the discrepancies. Those who initiated inquiries with the site's historical guides were provided with an information sheet outlining the project. However, the inserted objects were left unlabelled and unidentified.

Purchasing antique reproductions of pioneer housewares and Victoriana from a dozen Canadian and United States mail order catalogues and on-line merchandisers — such as the Bombay Company, Signals, and Lee Valley Tools — Ziegler created an energized environment which challenged viewers' knowledge of history and material culture. The interloping objects intensified the experience of the rooms, demanding close scrutiny to determine every object's "authentic" character. Whether it was a wire basket, copper lantern, swan decoy, porcelain flower arranger, block patch quilt or set of apothecary jars, distinguishing the "real" from

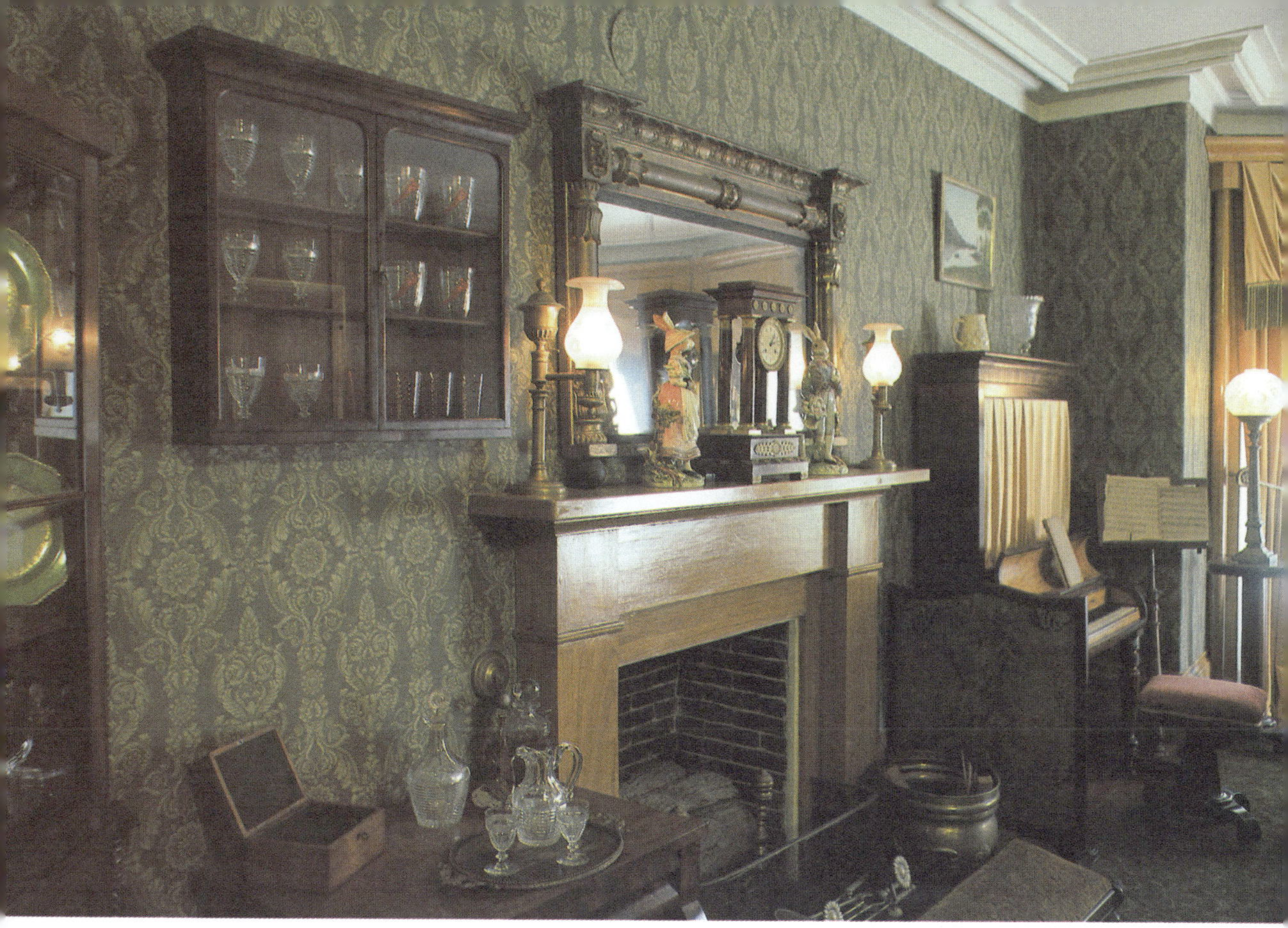

Mel Ziegler, installation view, *Mail Order Authenticity* 2001

"look-alike" required an expertise that exceeded the knowledge of most visitors. Even museum personnel with intimate knowledge of the collection were at times stumped. Obviously incongruous items such as Post-It notes and an executive golf putter set in the study, or an electric guitar in the drawing room, triggered a sense that something was seriously amiss in the historical purity of the *mise-en-scène*. Other objects resonated with autobiographical references. A Stetson on the hat rack and a set of tumblers emblazoned with chili peppers suggested Ziegler's home in Texas, while a frog-shaped rug and plastic rubber duckie (reportedly "on-loan" from his one-year-old twin sons) alluded to the artist's young family. Other items hinted at the secrets that permeate the domestic history of the period, such as the Victoria's Secret camisole in the maid's bedroom which provided a clue to the personal lives of nineteenth-century household servants, which are for the most part unrecorded.

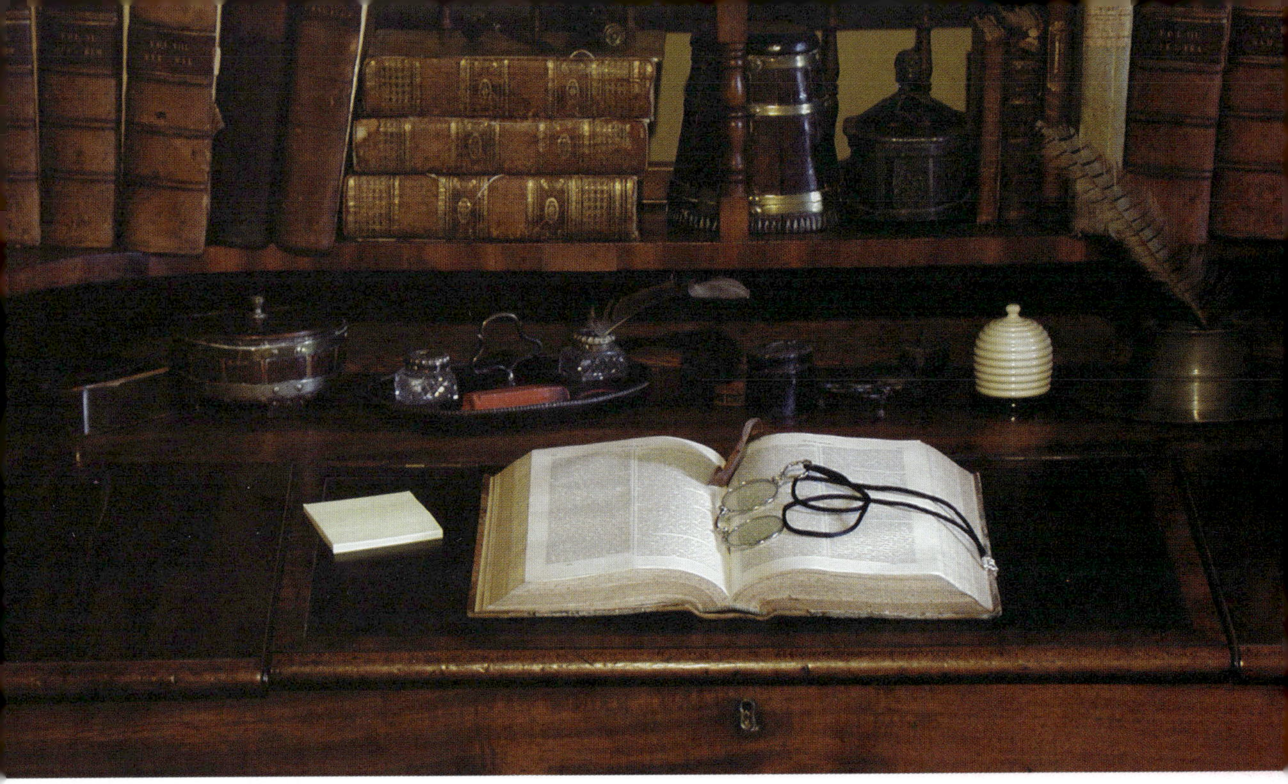

On one level, Ziegler's intervention invested an educational and sacralized site with mischievous possibilities. Since few of the objects on view at the site actually belonged to the first Prime Minister, the artist's "improper" objects interrupted the smooth admiration of historical accuracy and inspired speculation about what is known — and what can never be known — about the life of Sir John A. Macdonald: his taste in decoration, what heirlooms he may have accumulated and cherished, how the furnishings reflected his manner of being a husband and father, receiving guests, spending leisure time, and so on. On another level, Ziegler's faux-artifacts alluded to the artificiality endemic to the creation and display of history. If reproductions are as credible as originals, and dissimilar artifacts can be posed as a convincing ensemble, to what degree are constructed historical narratives likewise dependent upon simulated and fabricated totalities?

Mail Order Authenticity implicated more than just museum displays and their governing narratives. The trade in history and historicity carries both political and affective influence in diverse regions of popular culture: from *The Antiques Roadshow*'s treasure hunt mentality to landmark preservation campaigns, from Martha Stewart's style-training to living history museums' mixture of entertainment

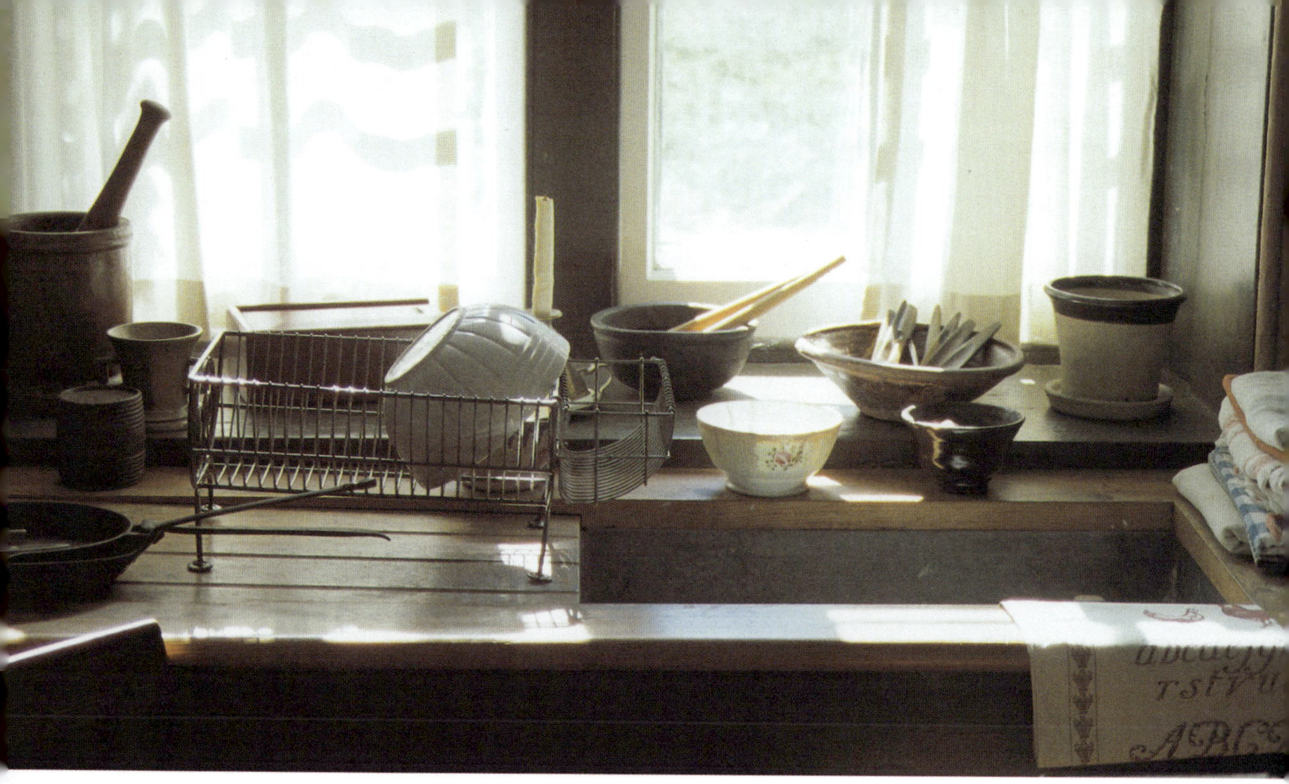

and nostalgia. The fact that advertisements in contemporary mail-order catalogues now mimic museum period rooms tellingly conflates the desire for commodities with the yearning for stability and continuity with the past. Ziegler's intervention highlighted the often uncanny similarities between museums, homes and catalogues, and exposed how objects can simultaneously embody multiple sorts of value — be it historical, pecuniary, stylistic or symbolic.

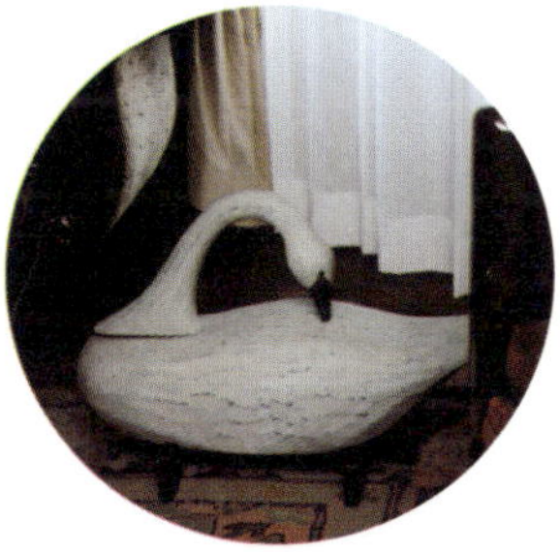

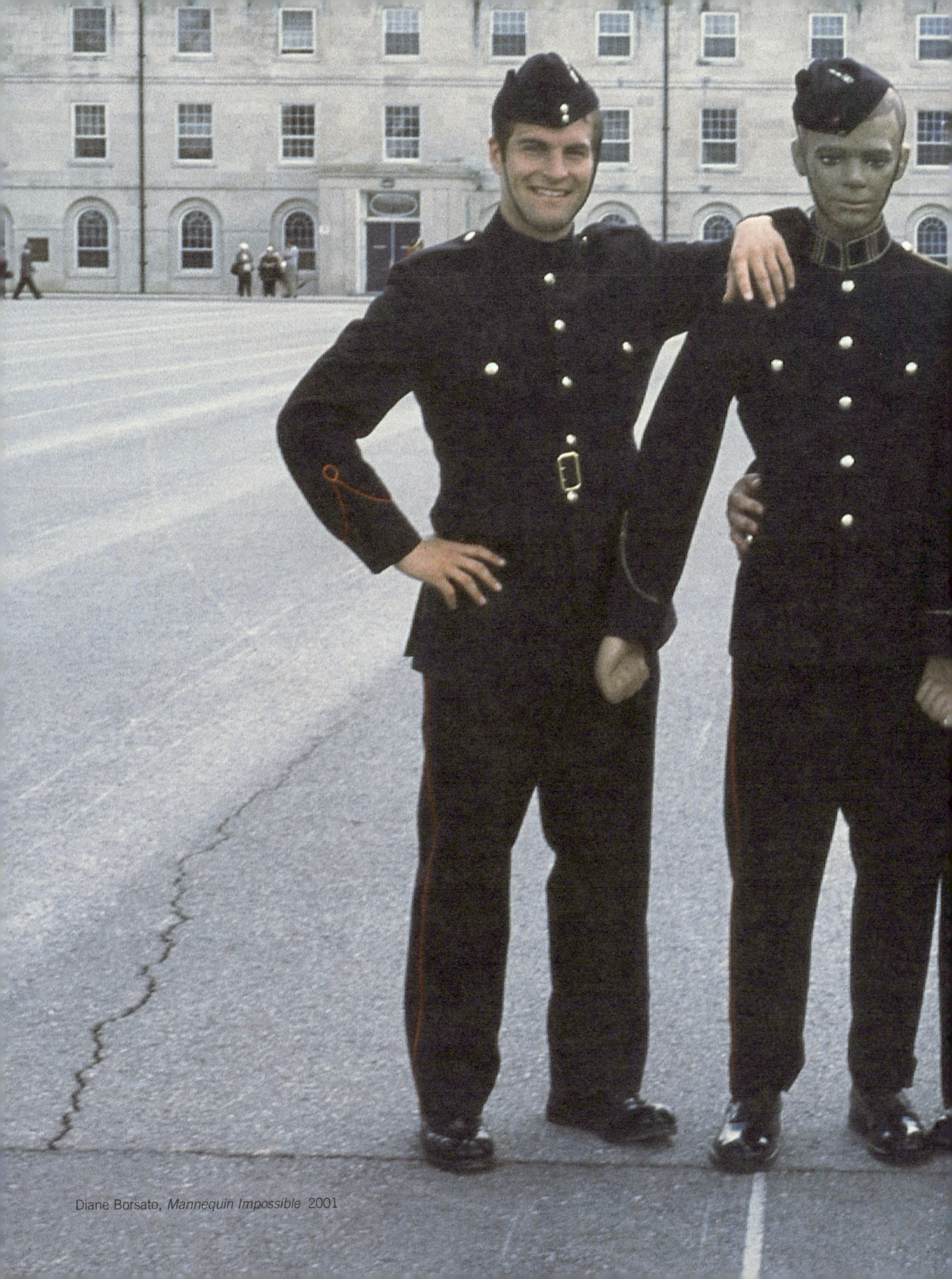

Diane Borsato, *Mannequin Impossible* 2001

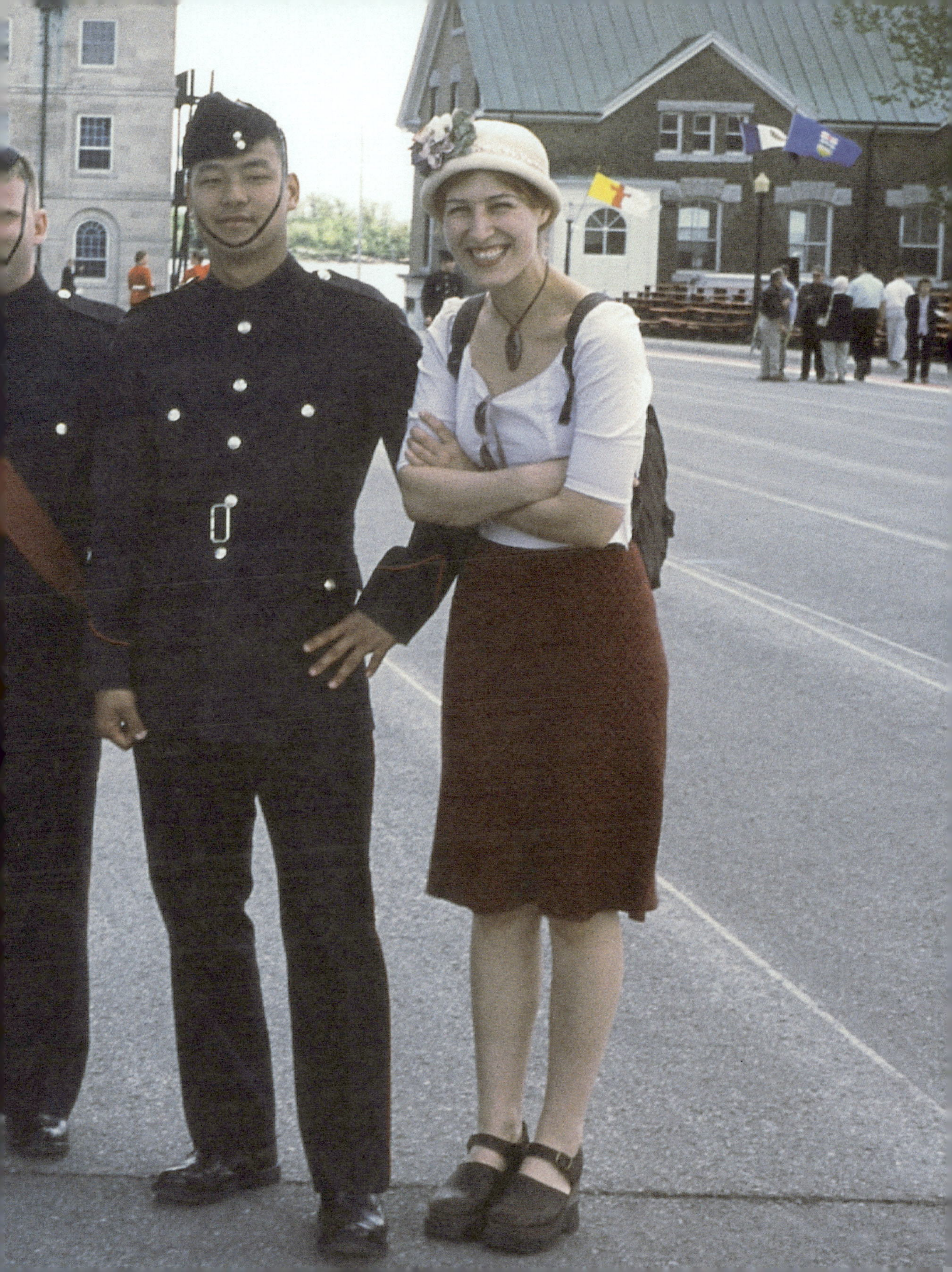

EMPATHOLOGY

Jim Drobnick and Jennifer Fisher

AS A MEDIUM OF COMMUNICATION, the exhibition is a distinctly ambulatory form: that is, its content must be enacted in order to be understood.[1] Museums, then, are more than just containers for showcasing objects; they are also sites of performance. Museumgoing, the paradigmatic act of aesthetic experience, comprises a number of secular rituals where audiences adapt their demeanour to and incorporate conventions from the cultivated manners of a knowledgable class.[2] During the nineteenth century, social advocates proclaimed their intentions to utilize museums performatively as a civilizing influence upon the behaviours (and hence the morals) of burgeoning urban populations.[3] Not only were visits to these institutions designed to formalize ways of looking, thinking and appreciation, but also those habits existing on the more corporeal level of emoting, acting and comportment. The fact that, when entering a museum, one immediately adopts a quieter, more restrained, contemplative mode of conduct attests to the continuing power of art's ideology and its capacity to operate on a nearly involuntary level upon the bodies of spectators.

EMPATHOLOGY extended the examination of museums and collecting foregrounded in the installations of MUSEOPATHY into the performative dimension. Composed of four performances staged at MUSEOPATHY's sites, EMPATHOLOGY artists enlivened the fixed displays of these museums with subjective encounters at times surreal, disjunctive, confrontational or humorous. These vital interventions offered an alternative "embodied" means for generating æsthetic experience and historical knowledge by reorienting the audience interaction typical to each site.

As the title of this performance series suggested, an interest in the phenomenon of empathy predominated, especially as it served as the vehicle of auratic affect. Whereas sympathy, as Susan Buck-Morss elucidates, renders in the beholder a state of being simulateously affected, to "feel the same," empathy is the ability to profoundly understand a state of another quite different from the self, in other words, to "feel across difference."[4] Hence EMPATHOLOGY aimed to create moments of identification that bridged radically distinct museological and performative cultures.

Each performance set up an affectual encounter by engaging artifacts, museum contexts and audiences in specific interactions. The context-sensitive[5] events of EMPATHOLOGY solicited beholders to engage with a range of museologically induced feeling states. The four performances reflected upon and responded to the diverse layers of institutional resonances. Intentionally contravening the unspoken rules of museum demeanour, the artists ate and drank in the museum, talked pointedly about the objects and visitors, touched artworks or dramatically over-emoted. Proposing new models of exchange between visitors and artifacts in the case of Diane Borsato and Peter Hobbs, or between artist and audience with Linda Montano and Clive Robertson, these events reconceived the museum as a zone of interaction and nascent affinities.

NOTES

1. See Jennifer Fisher, *Aesthetic Contingencies: Relational Enactments in Display Culture*, Ph.D. Dissertation, Montreal: Concordia University, 1995; and Barbara Kirshenblatt-Gimblett, *Destination Culture: Tourism, Museums, and Heritage*, Berkeley: University of California Press, 1998.
2. See Carol Duncan, *Civilizing Rituals: Inside Public Art Museums*, New York and London: Routledge, 1995.
3. See Tony Bennett, *The Birth of the Museum: History, Theory, Politics*, New York and London: Routledge, 1995.
4. Grant Kester and Susan Buck-Morss, "Aesthetics After the End of Art: An Interview with Susan Buck-Morss," *Art Journal* 56:1, Spring 1997, p. 40.
5. "Context sensitive," is a term coined by Marysia Lewandowska and Neil Cummings, "chance projects: from browser to gift," paper presented at the conference *In Public*, organized by Joan Borsa, April 2001, Montreal.

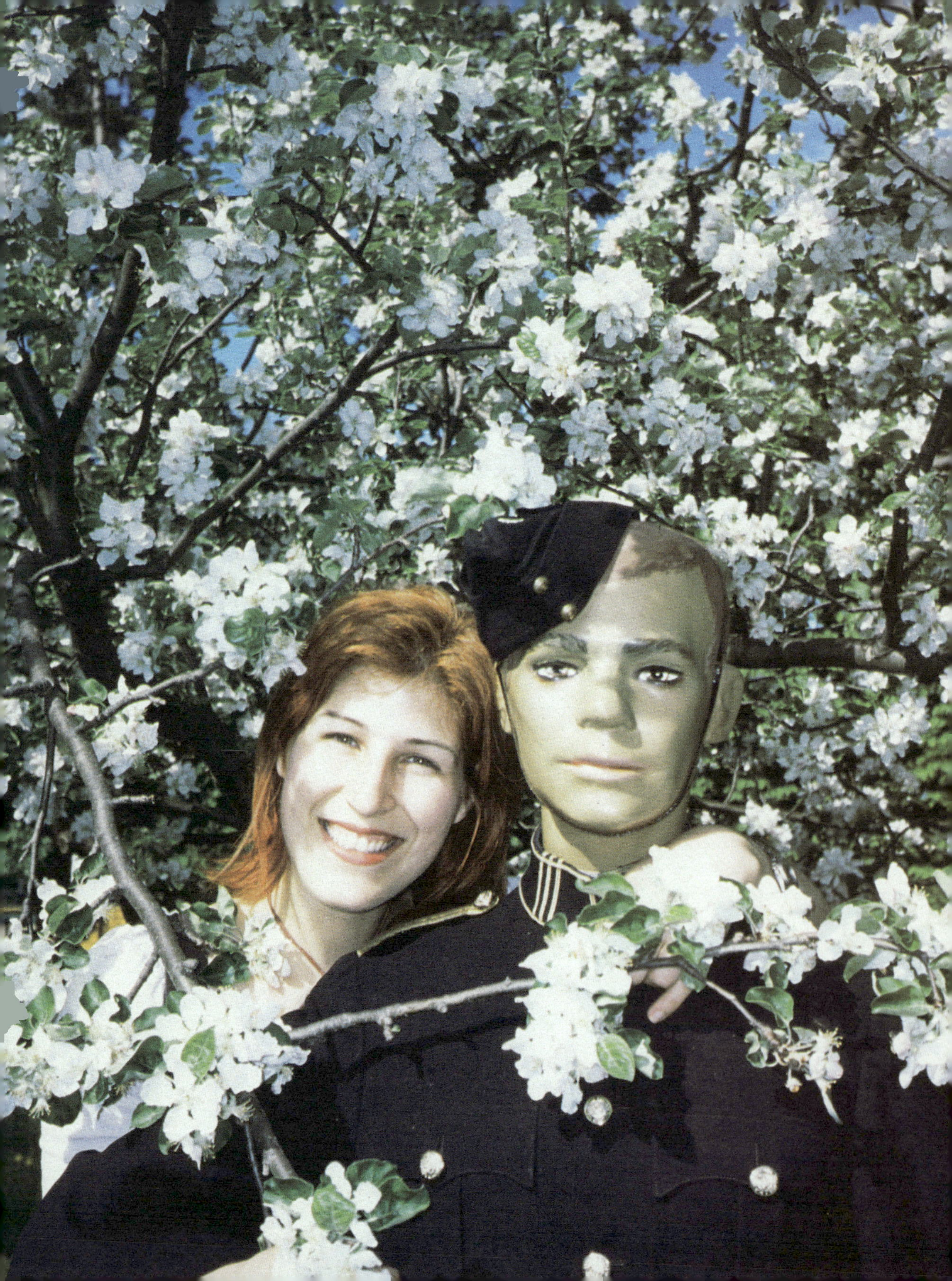

DIANE BORSATO

Royal Military College of Canada Museum

FOR MORE THAN THREE DECADES, "Mortimer" has stood in the entrance of the Royal Military College of Canada Museum clad in a blue officer-cadet uniform representing the typical RMC student. Dusty with time and taunted by visiting schoolchildren, the 1940s era mannequin seemed forgotten by history. In *Mannequin Impossible*, Diane Borsato honoured the stalwart effigy with attention and fresh air. Taking him out of the museum for the first time and into the formal celebrations of the RMC's Graduation Weekend, Borsato escorted Mortimer on a number of adventures on campus and around the city: attending graduation ceremonies, meeting with military families and officials, marching in a parade, visiting romantic vistas and smoky barrooms, and even going to the Prom.

In previous works, Borsato has adopted idiosyncratic practices of exploring the subject of love and the mythologies of romance. Unusual but disciplined methods have included sleeping with cake, touching strangers, boiling sentimental objects, and living in the gallery while trying to give herself back massages — all in the service of seeking ways to experience affection, achieve comfort and instigate self-transformation. Borsato's approach to performance is often highly sensory and forthrightly intimate, and her project for EMPATHOLOGY continues this logic by setting up an inquiry into the meaning of the artifact by not just by holding and looking at it, or by researching provenance, but by *loving* it. Taking an empathetic process to the ultimate degree — personifying the costumed artifact with the full gamut of feelings, hopes, desires and dreams — she appropriated the dating ritual as a research tool and simultaneously came to his (imagined) emotional rescue.

The use of the mannequin by Borsato inverted the gender dynamics of the classical Pygmalion myth, for here it was a woman's yearning that animated the statue. As well, the performance contravened the use of mannequins by male artists such as the Surrealists of the 1930s and '40s (and their latent misogyny) and by *enfants terribles* in the 1990s (and their penchant for shock and abjection). Borsato's

Diane Borsato, *Mannequin Impossible* 2001

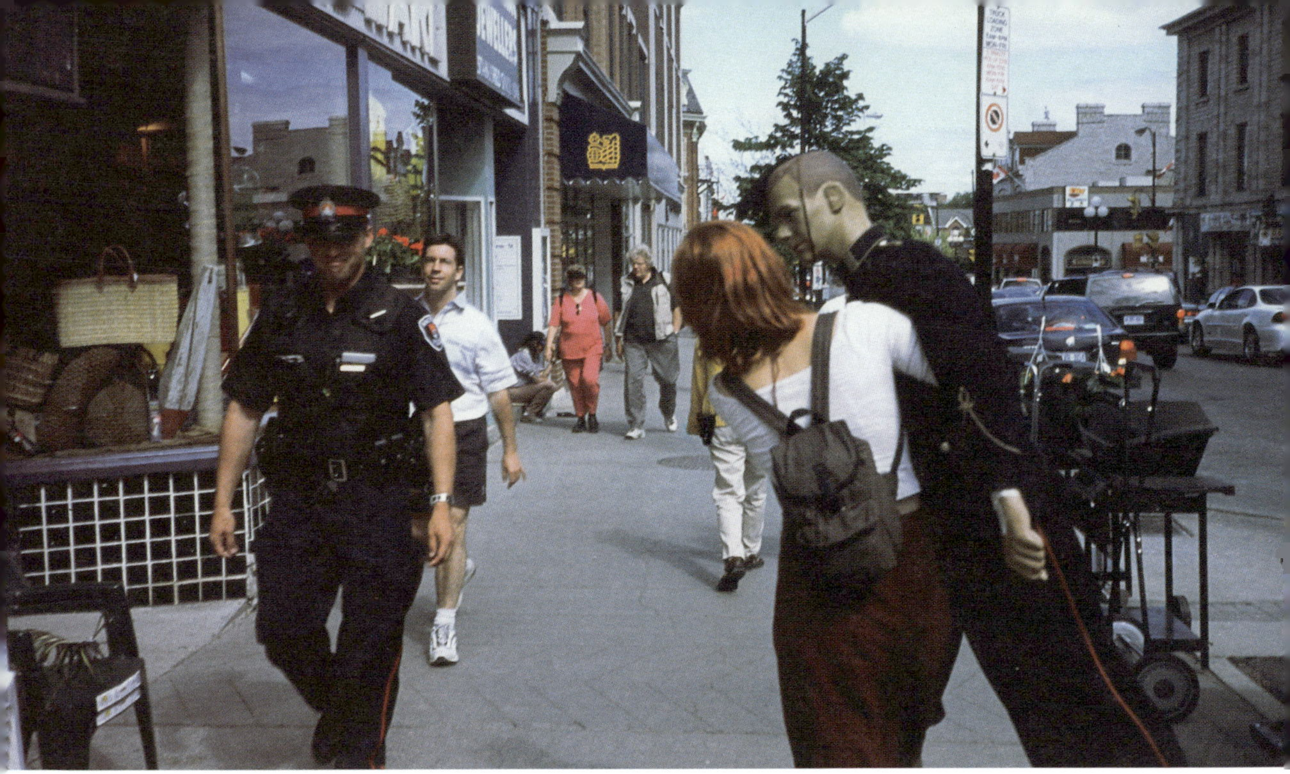

aims were more compassionate: to ennoble the plaster likeness by allowing him to experience the social aspects of college life and to fulfil the rites of cadet training. There was a sense that the dyad of prom-dressed woman and uniformed man harkened back to the era of WWII romances, when military/civilian flirtations formed a previous generation's personal history of coming of age. The universal embrace of the artist and her date by military personnel, tourists and townfolk alike — as they strolled down streets, posed in front of tanks or crashed parades and parties — confirmed the familiarity of this trope and superseded any intimations of the uncanny that emerge when artists utilize mannequins.

The popular appeal of the duo continued at the opening of MUSEOPATHY, when Borsato showed slides and shared stories of her and Mortimer's escapades, as she served cake to visitors on the RMC Museum's gun platform. Mixing the formality of an artist's talk with the conviviality of showing home movies, she made herself charmingly approachable among 32-pounder guns and cannonballs. Hallmark card-like images of Borsato and Mortimer's date included watching a sunset, eating ice cream cones, walking among blossoming trees and sitting on a bench overlooking the lake.

The emphasis on romance notwithstanding, Borsato's performance enacted a subtle form of gender subversion and critique of masculinity. The rigid and inert figure had its authority inadvertently compromised when carried about, hoisted up by the crotch or split at the waist to fit into a car. Within Kingston the number of obscene jokes and gestures made by passersby indicated that the couple's spectacle was received in the genre of military and college pranks. As the allusion to television's 1960s Cold War thriller series suggests, *Mannequin Impossible* was a cover for a spy mission. Traditionally, the military has defined itself outside the domain of female desire. Fortresses are designed to withstand assault, but can they withstand affection? After his rendezvous, Mortimer returned to duty in the museum with a red lipstick kiss on his cheek.

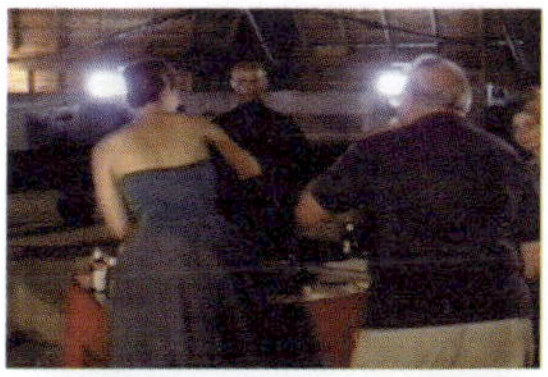
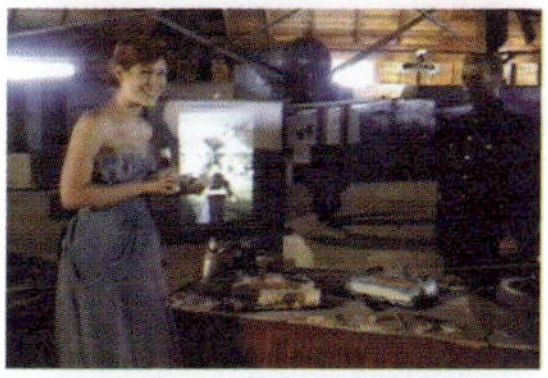
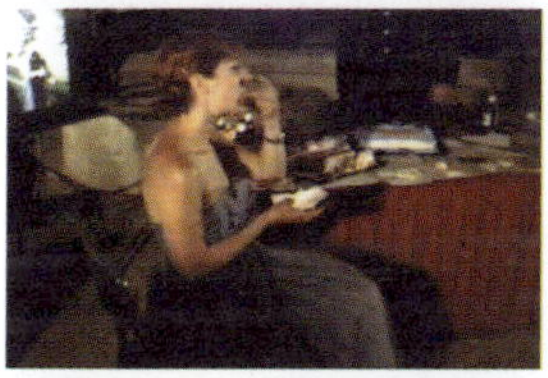
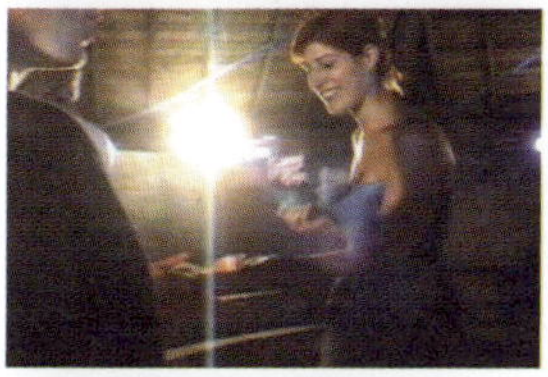
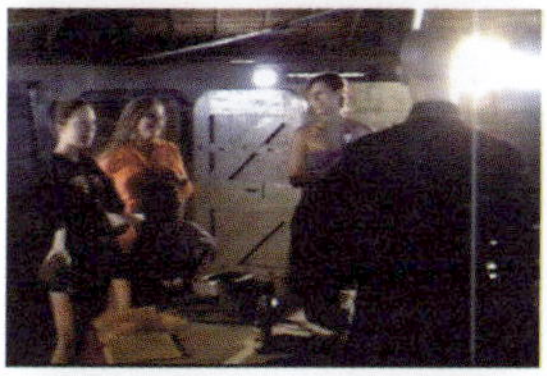
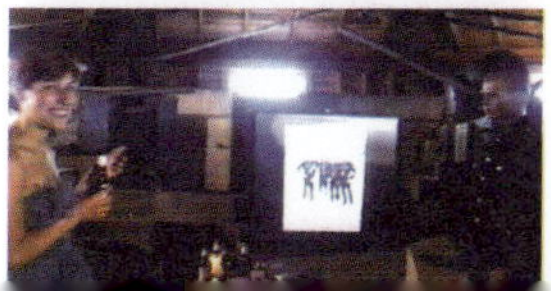
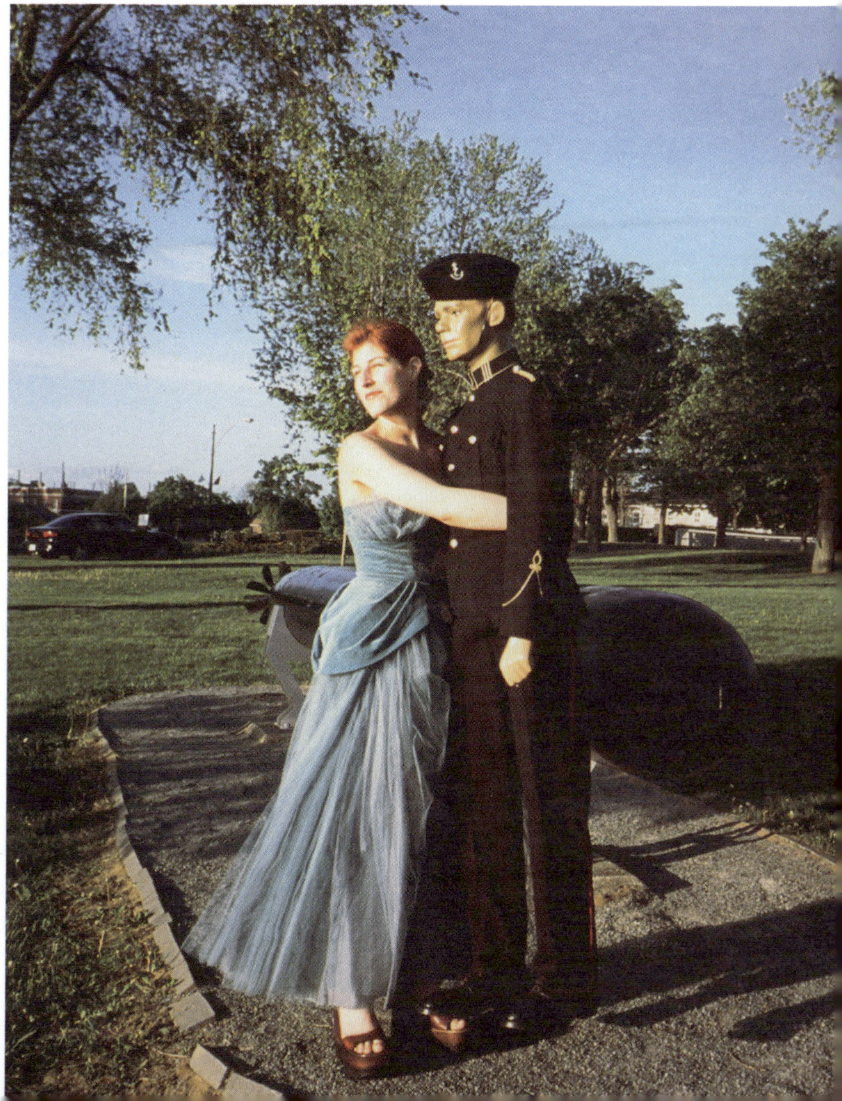

PETER HOBBS

Bellevue House National Historic Site

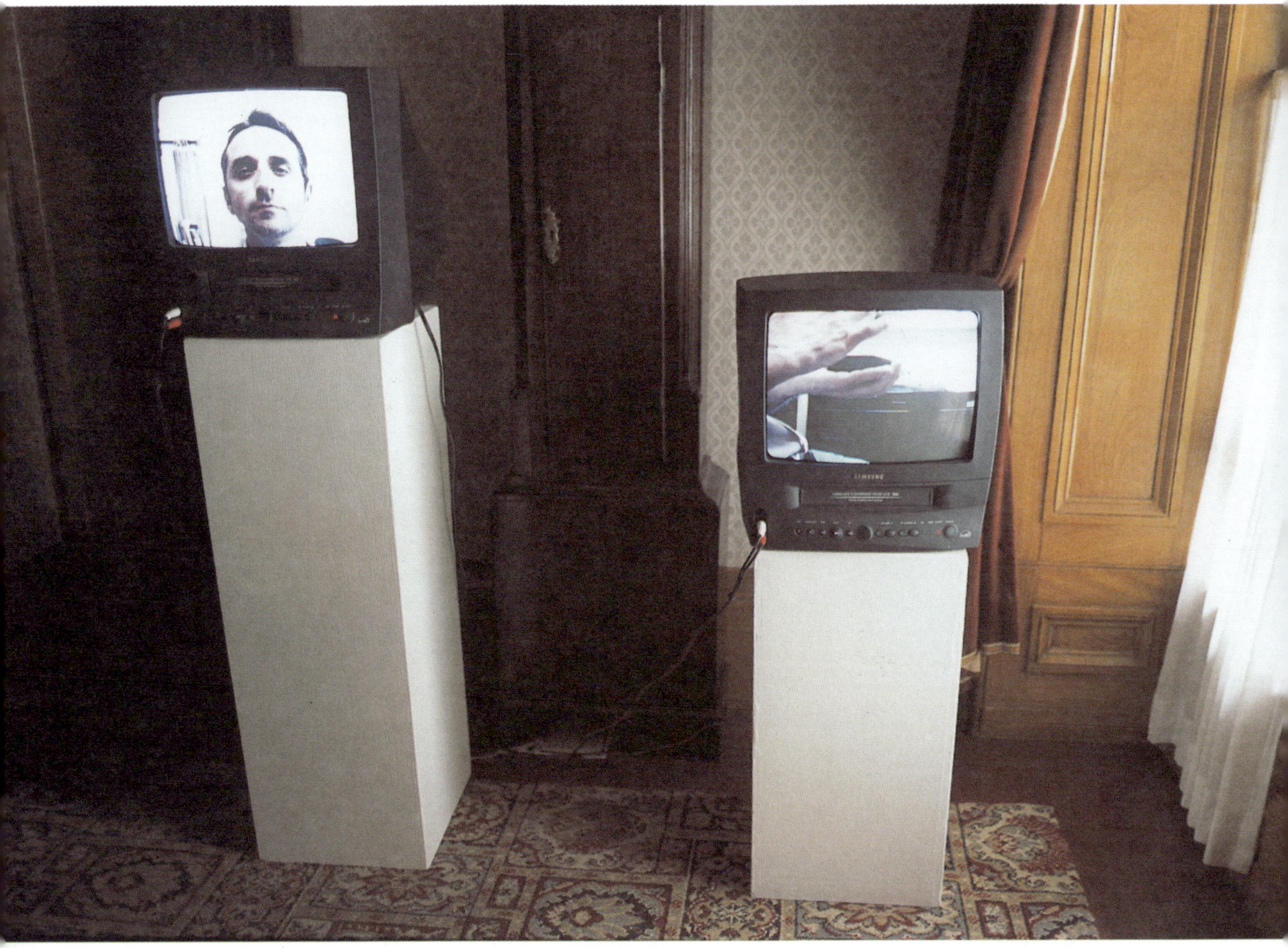

Peter Hobbs, installation view
and stills from video, *Gothic* 2001

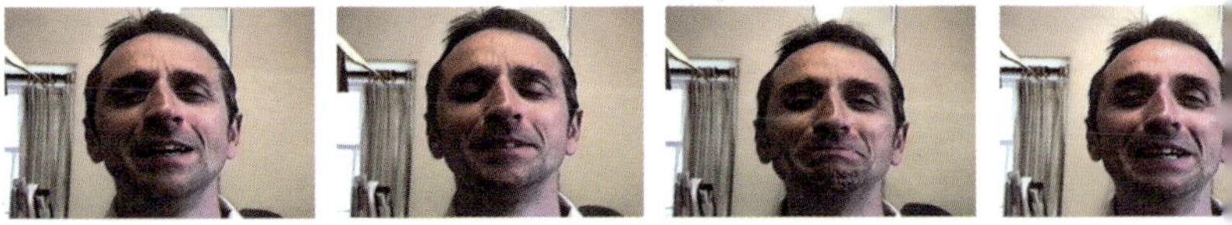

MUSEUMS OFTEN STRATEGICALLY APPEAL TO VISITORS' SENTIMENTS, and in this performance, *Gothic*, Peter Hobbs took up the idea of empathy literally. Stirred by the stories narrated by the guides and wall texts at Bellevue House relating to the prolonged illness afflicting Isabella, Sir John A. Macdonald's wife, and the death of their infant son, the artist attempted to express the emotional affect permeating the site and embodied in its objects.

Secluded in a room off-limits to visitors, Hobbs sat in a chair holding and caressing period objects — such as a hairpin, bath sponge, toothbrush, and tea cup — from the Bellevue House collection. With one camera framing his hands, and the other fixed upon his face, houseguests were able to view the artist from two monitors placed on the landing in the central stairwell. Like the stairs which form a transitional link between the downstairs public rooms and the upstairs private areas, the objects handled by Hobbs were mobilized as connectors — between nineteenth and twenty-first centuries, the world of historical personages and present-day tourists.

Playing off the word "aura" in both its sense of historical value and psychical presence, Hobbs tested the mysterious powers of objects to evoke sensations. While not claiming to possess supernatural powers, he nevertheless adopted a psychometric approach to otherworldly communion with the feeling-states in which the objects were once immersed. Searching to transform his understanding

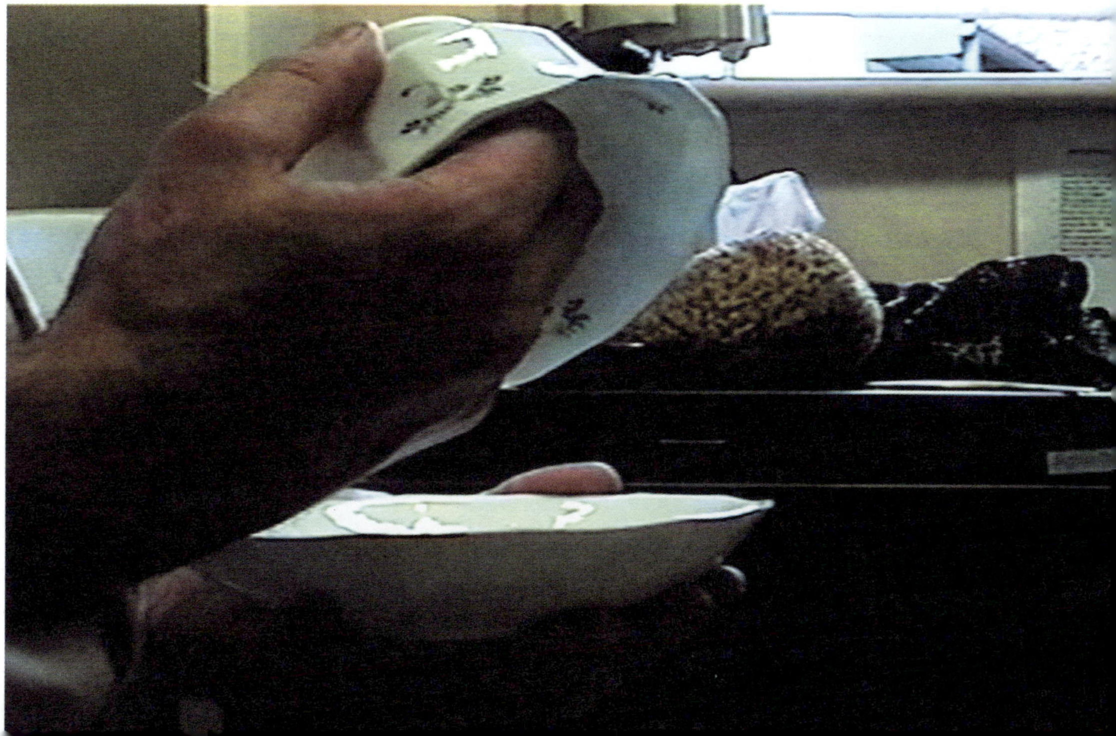

of the historical significance of the site from one based on visual intellection into one founded on tactile alignment with emotional resonances, he risked the experience of an altered state. The live video provided compelling evidence of his trance-like attention, his use of focusing and breathing techniques and his laboured grimacing and sweating. Afterwards, Hobbs related that despite his conscious preparation and expectant attitude, he felt hit by a forceful wave of emotion that was disturbing as well as surprising. His limbs went numb, he thought he was going to pass out, and he wept uncontrollably.

For those growing up Protestant in Upper Canada in the 1960s, crying was not part of the conventional male emotional repertoire. Hobbs challenged proper museum conduct as well as his own acculturated sense of emotional propriety and the cultural taboo which dictates that, for men, weeping in public is a sign of unforgivable weakness. While men have noticeably cried as a melodramatic plot device or in various media spectacles (post-September 11 news coverage featured a number of such prominent images), the risk of appearing unmanly still hovers over men displaying vulnerability and heart-rending sentiments.

For a number of writers, museums are inextricably coupled with melancholy and mourning, and many of the museums and heritage sites in Kingston, especially those associated with hospitals, prisons and commemorative war monuments, bear more than a passing association with grief and sadness. At Bellevue House, a home in which misfortune haunts an already dark Victorian-era ambiance, a prevailing

Bellevue House

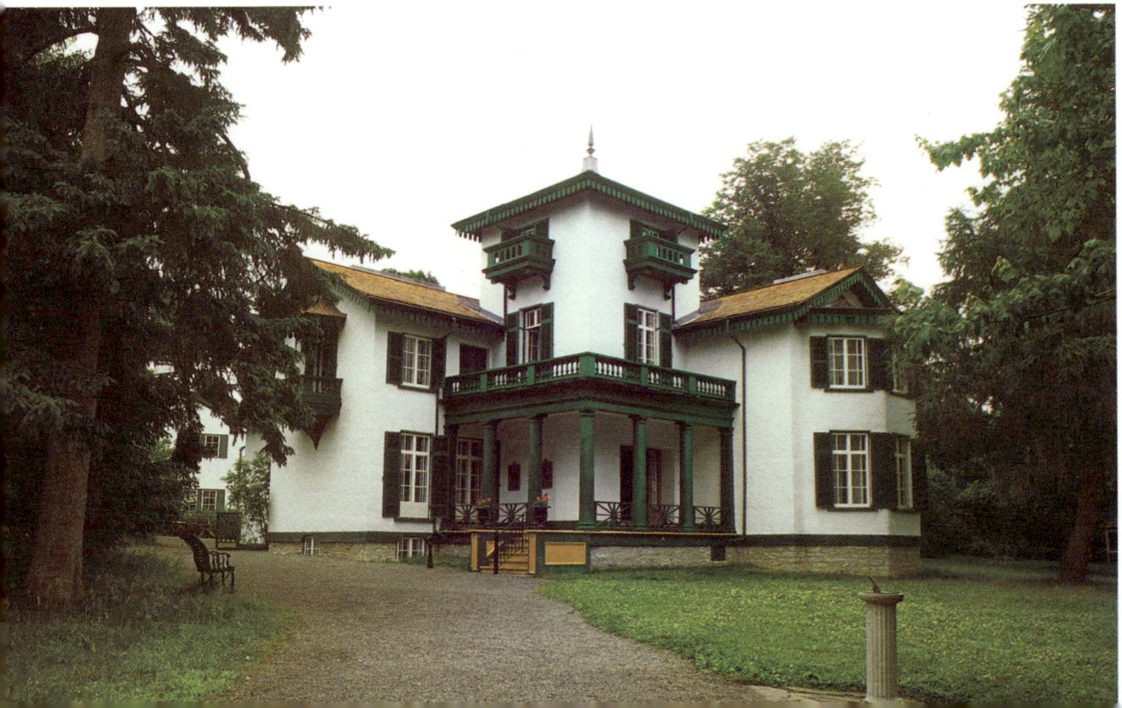

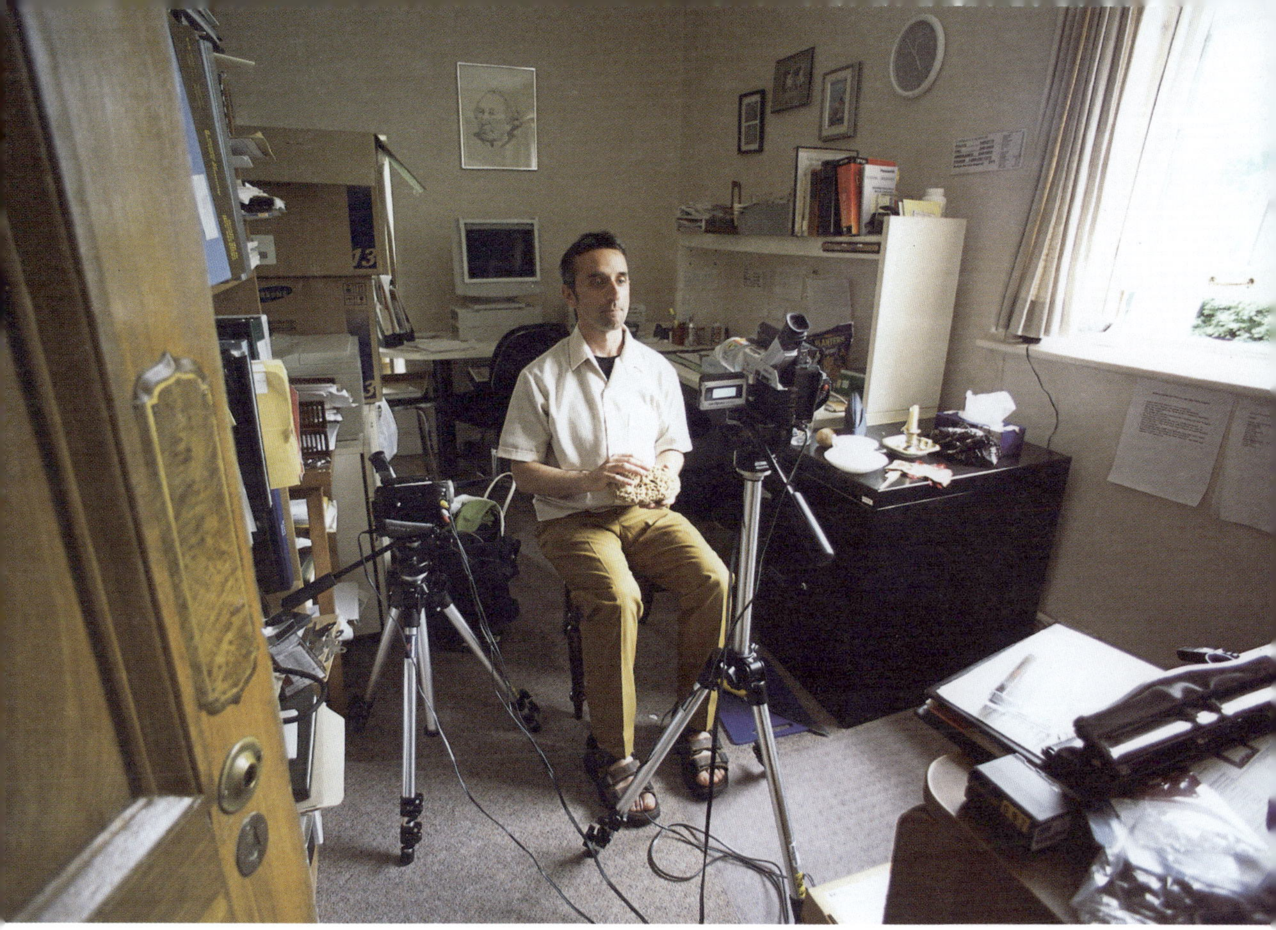

Peter Hobbs, view from behind the scenes, *Gothic* 2001

sense of tragedy looms. Hobbs' performance, more than just an exercise in mordancy or paranormal chic, memorialized the mood present in the decor and narratives of the site, and embraced the thanatopic sensibility defining the previous fin-de-siècle. The Gothic mien alluded to in the work's title referred less to the macabre and the sepulchral than to Victorian grieving rituals satisfying yearnings to communicate with the "other side" through seances and Ouija boards, and the fetishistic preservation of the relics of deceased loved ones. Hobbs' ritual crying went further than just complementing the Victoriana of Bellevue House; it personalized and physicalized its dominant emotional tenor, one hundred and fifty years after the fact.

LINDA MONTANO

Museum Ship ALEXANDER HENRY

THROUGHOUT HER CAREER, Linda Montano has merged the presumably distinct domains of art and life in compelling and pioneering performances. Over the past few years her art has increasingly featured therapeutic concerns, especially involving the dedicated care of other individuals, stemming from the artist's choice to look after her 88-year-old father, Henry. Drawing on her life experience as a novice for the Maryknoll nuns, her subsequent study of yoga, and longstanding practice of performance art, she converted a nautical interior into a retreat for the navigation of personal exculpation. Compassion and self-empowerment combined in a public reconciliation ritual that provided a model for their integration into one's everyday life.

Forgiveness as Art was staged within the largest artifact in the collection of the Marine Museum of the Great Lakes — the 3,000-ton Museum Ship *Alexander Henry*. For the performance, Montano and her collaborator, Jessica Wyman, occupied the VIP quarters on the Promenade Deck and extended the function of "secular cleric" conventionally reserved for a ship's captain who performs the rites of marriage or burying the dead. Amidst the suite's decor of marine paintings, nautical mementos and portraits of the Queen, with portholes overlooking the ship's bow and the Marine Museum itself, a forgiveness ambiance was created to foster relaxation and self-examination. *Forgiveness as Art* constructed a ritualistic enclave in the gently rocking ship to enable participants to contemplate, experience and (perchance) to share forgiveness.

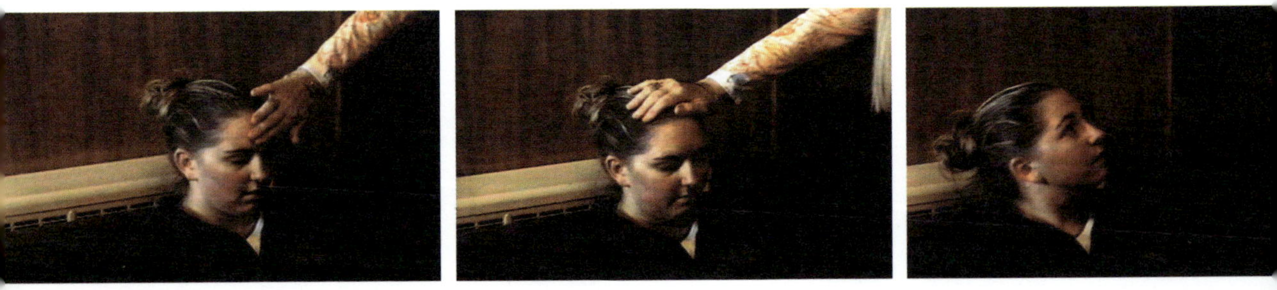

Linda Montano, performance stills, *Forgiveness as Art* 2001

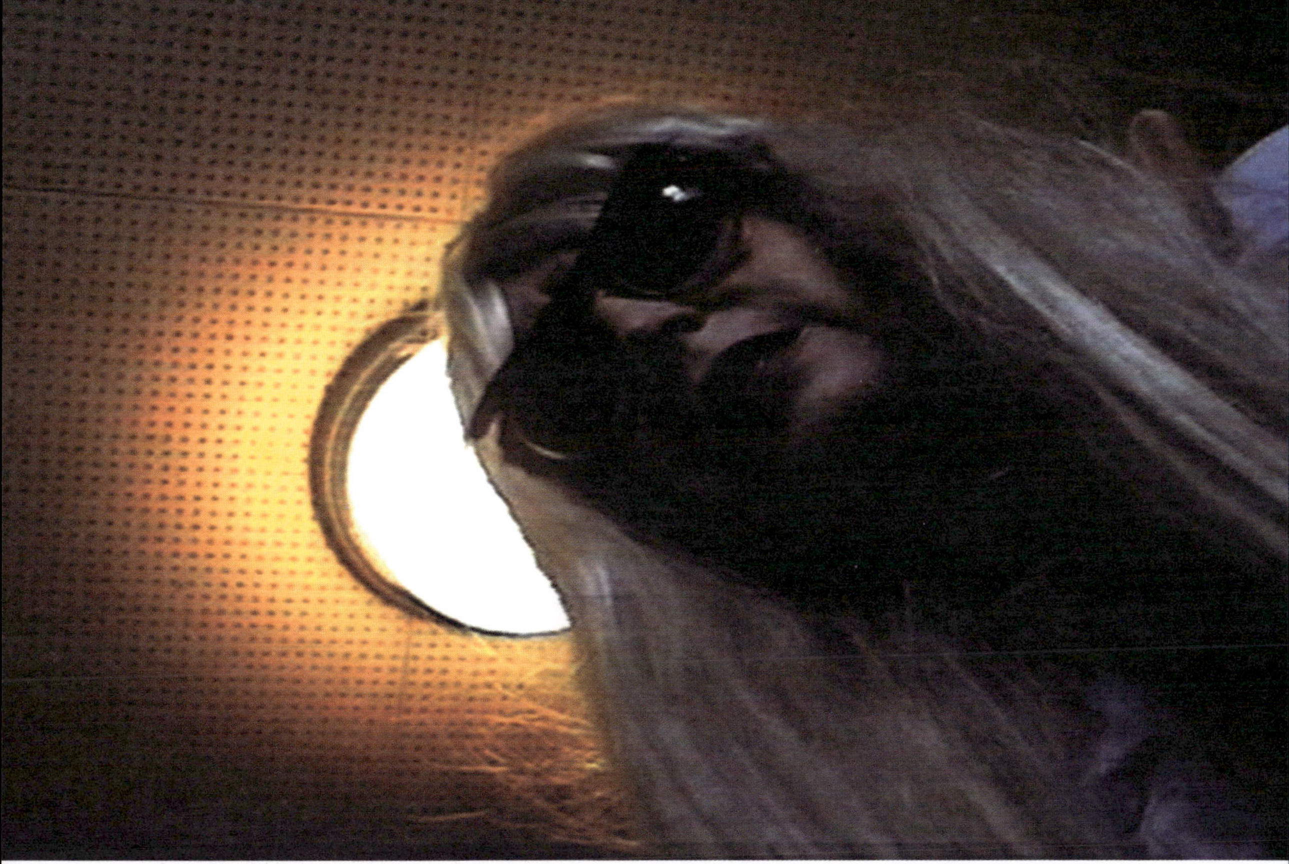

Participants were first greeted by Montano and Wyman dressed colourfully in Forgiveness Girl drag — campy wigs, sunglasses and red *bindi*s between their eyebrows, a signifier of sanctity and ascetism in yogic culture. The exaggerated costumes, at once carnivalesque and absurd, utilized humour to defuse pretensions towards sanctimoniousness yet announced that the bedrooms and lounge of the cabin had been christened with a heightened sense of alterity and liminality. The music of Jackie Gleason and his orchestra reverberated quietly in the rooms as the audience read the guidelines for the simple series of manoeuvres: 1. Write something you want to forgive about yourself or someone else; 2. Bring the paper into the Forgiveness Rooms; 3. Lay down or sit for three to four minutes and feel forgiveness; 4. Receive a forgiveness blessing from the Forgiveness Girls.

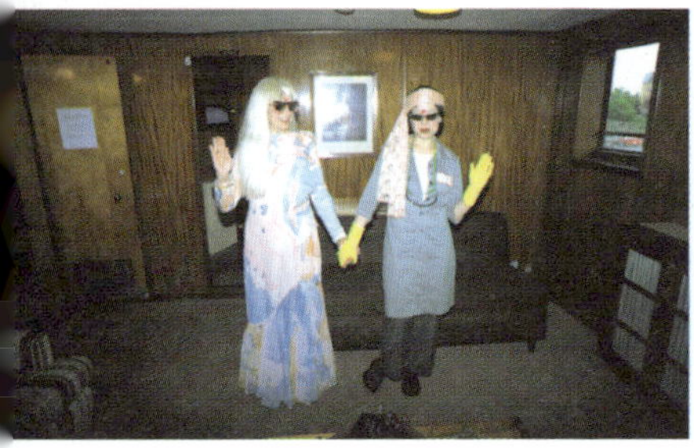

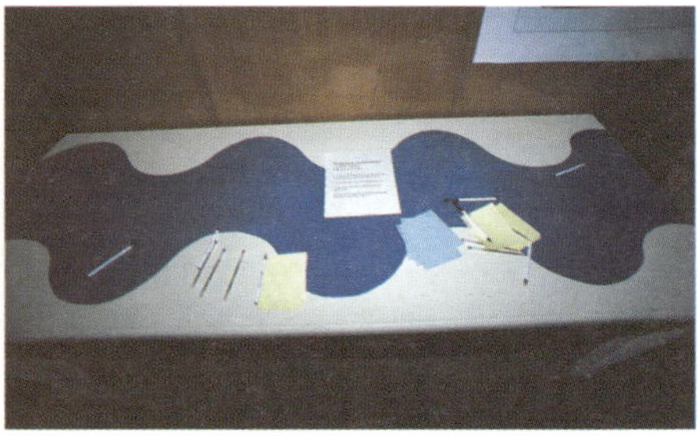

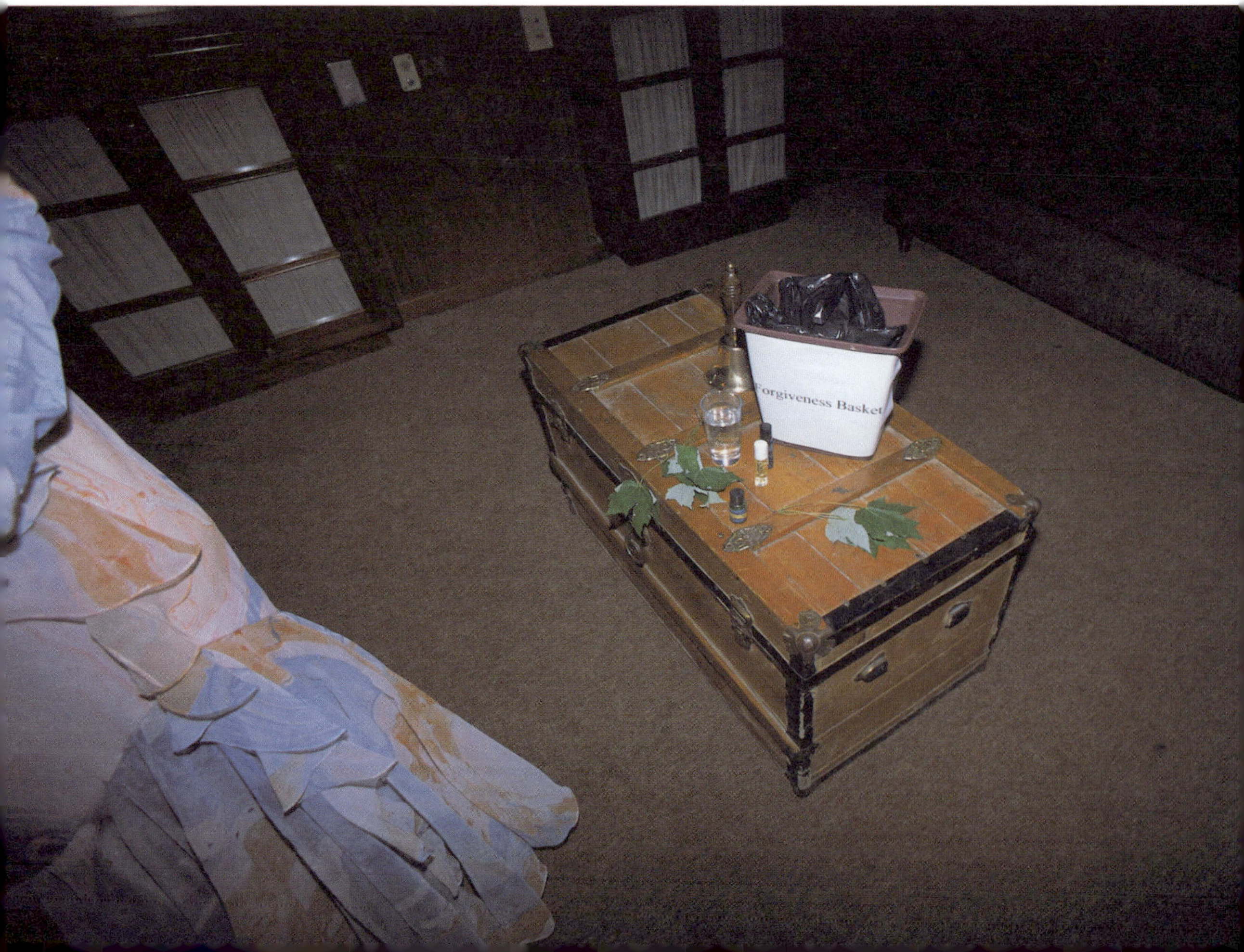
Forgiveness Basket

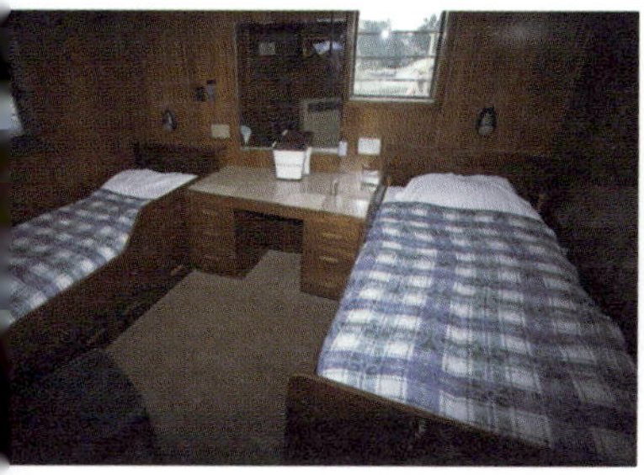

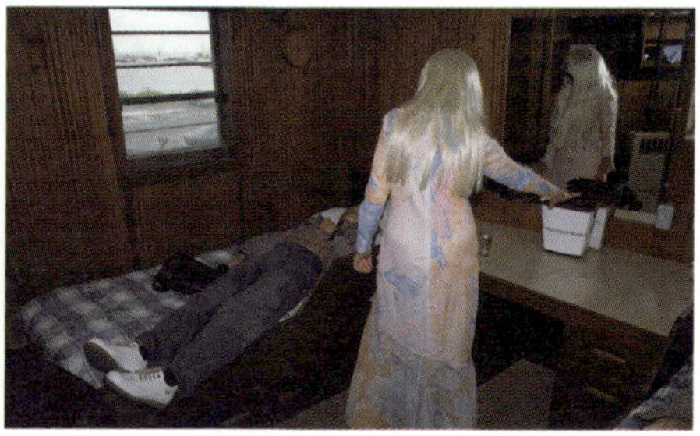

After musing and writing down their thoughts, participants relaxed on one of the bunks or chairs. They were instructed to close their eyes, remain quiet, hold the piece of paper close to their heart, and feel forgiveness. When the appropriate time had passed, Montano or Wyman asked visitors if they felt ready, and then absolved them with the statement: “You are forgiven. Continue to forgive yourself and to feel forgiveness.” With foreheads anointed by water or the aromatic oils of lavender, jasmine or rosemary, participants rose, tore up the paper and placed it in the Forgiveness Basket. A bell was rung to mark the completion of the rite and to signify the person’s graduation into a state of forgiveness.

Like navigational beacons, the personae of the Forgiveness Girls functioned to guide rather than to exonerate. The recuperative intention of the performance, akin to the procedure of confession, established a frame for receiving compassion. But because it took place outside the institutional authority of a church, such sentiments as guilt or embarrassment were greeted by amiable non-judgment rather than penitential protocols. Significantly, the agency of forgiveness was entrusted to participants themselves. They were told “You can repeat this for yourself or someone else at any time” and thus were offered a life management tool that could be used at their own discretion in future circumstances.

In public performances, especially ones that request visitors to examine personal or intimate issues, it is to be expected that some reluctance would emerge. More than a few visitors, however, advanced deeply into the therapeutic process, which seemingly caught them unaware. They lingered in the space, or later expressed to Montano and Wyman the unexpected power they experienced during the performance. Such responses foreground the effectiveness of even informal rituals, and the potential for art to function as, in Montano’s words, “a vehicle for harmony and wisdom.”

CLIVE ROBERTSON

MUSEOPATHY *Sites*

ADOPTING THE ROLE OF INTERVIEWER, Clive Robertson's performance *Speaking Tours* engaged an activity of "collecting" opinions about the site-specific installations comprising MUSEOPATHY. In a series of one-on-one conversations with art historians, artists, cultural theorists and other scholars, recorded while walking through each of the participating museums and heritage sites, he created an audio archive of responses generated by the interrelationship of artists, artworks and sites. Functioning simultaneously as an historian, educator, critic and artist, Robertson's subject position was complex and variable, one that extended his role as an instigator of critical thinking in the Canadian artistic community.

The conversational performances wryly downplayed the authority of the artist in a conceptual manoeuvre that emphasized the politics of listening and reception. Leading the speakers on a tour (without imposing a path), encouraging others to voice opinions and insights (while still devising the questions), the discussions went further than just serving as an exercise in art criticism and aesthetic evaluation. Instead, the "parallel commentaries" on the sites and interventions focused more on sightseeing, museums and, in Robertson's words, "the temporary historical and aesthetic restructurings and experiences offered up by the guest artists." More akin to a mode of sociological investigation, the dialogues tended to problematize reductivist notions of power, whether those of institutions, curators or artists, and to explore how the cultural practices of tourism, display, collecting, museums, and the functions of civic identity and public space converge and mutually influence each other.

The audience often became the subject of the conversations. At times Robertson and his guest assumed the role of plainclothes observers watching museumgoers. The viewing habits of MUSEOPATHY's "inadvertent audience" — those unexpectedly confronted by the artworks in the general course of a museum visit — contrasted sharply with art world individuals explicitly motivated to examine the artworks.

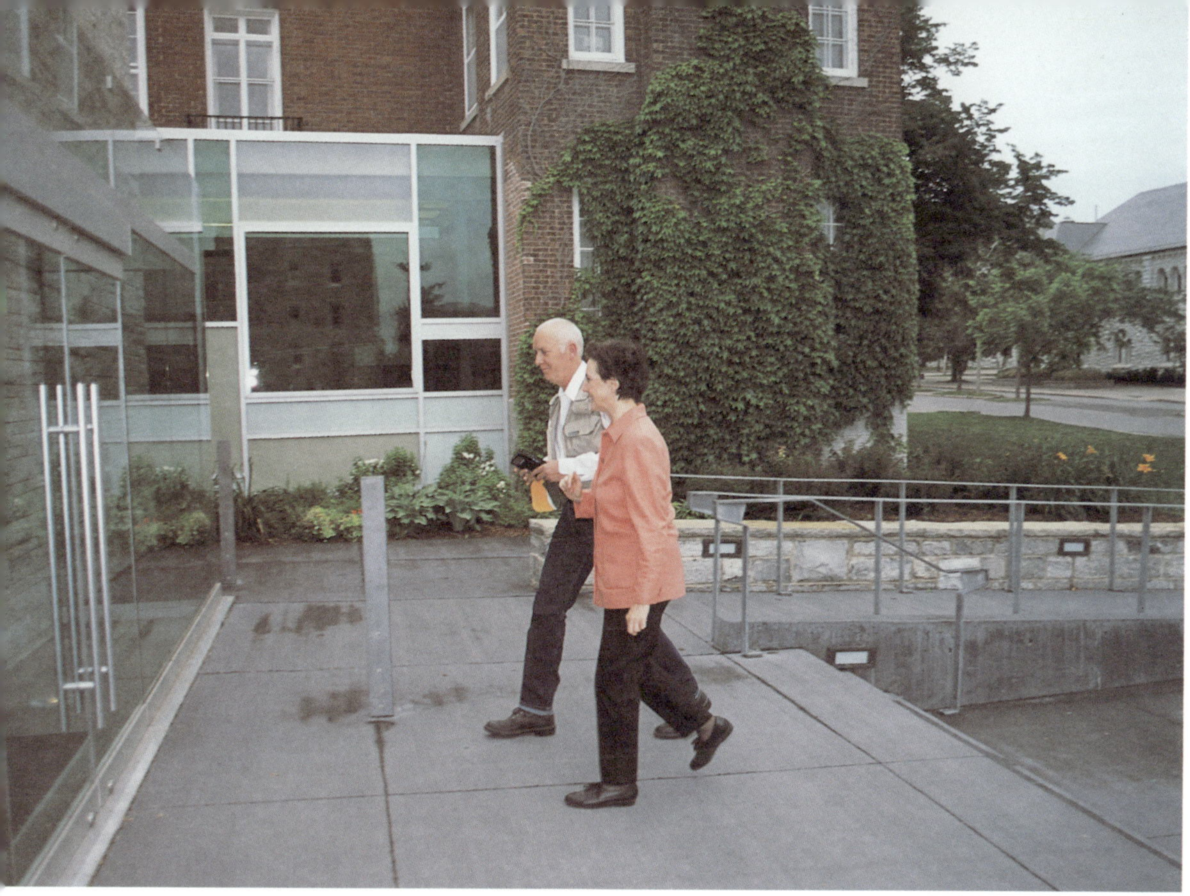

Clive Robertson, performance stills, *Speaking Tours* 2001

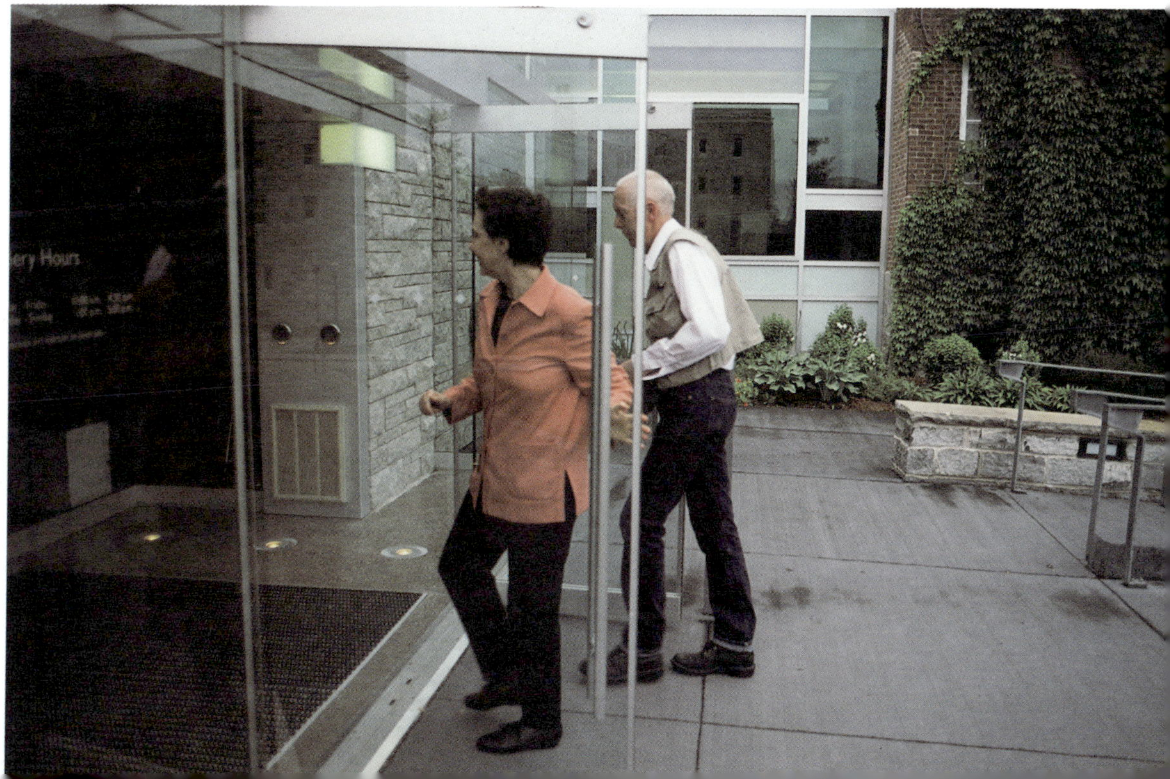

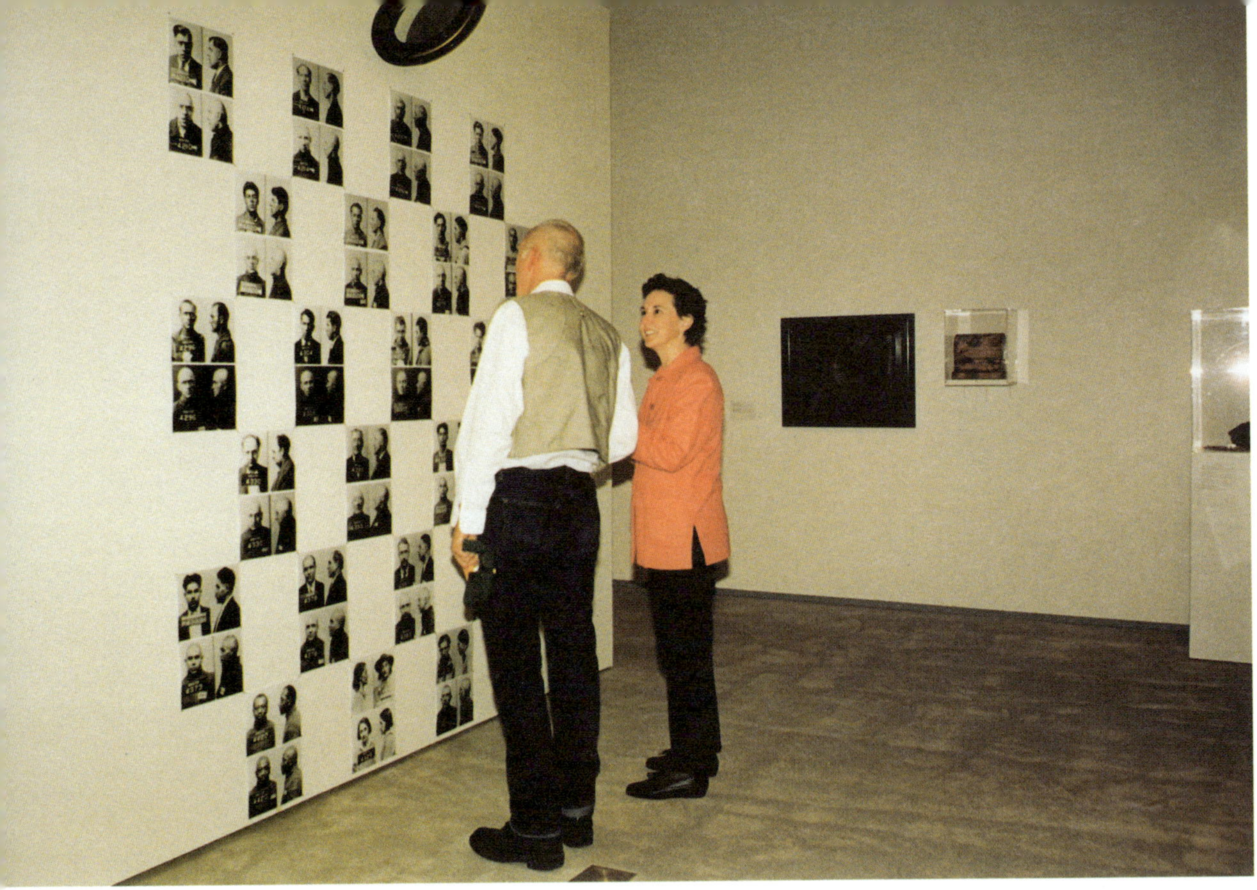

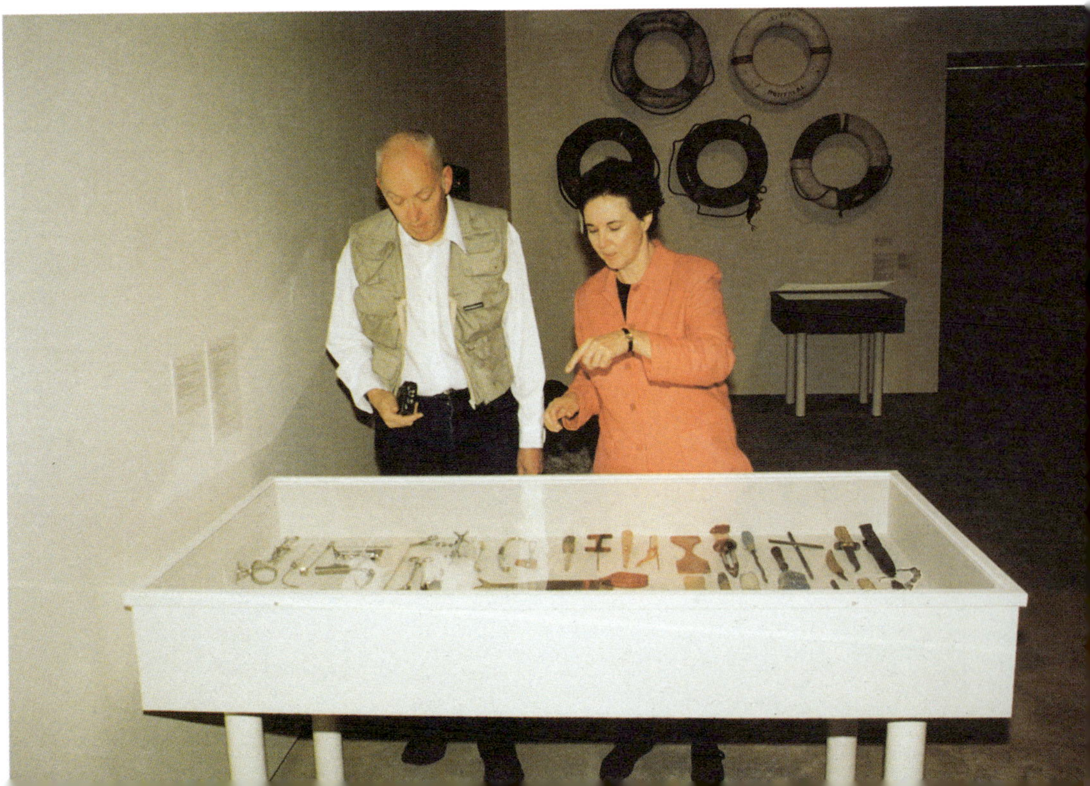

At the Marine Museum, for instance, discussion of aesthetic issues pertaining to John Dickson's *SOS* installation was superseded by animated concerns about the difficulty of ascertaining the optimal moment to photograph the bubbles as they broke the water's surface and converged to form their message.

Robertson's practice — whether written, performative or curatorial — involves a substantial research component, especially in regards to analyses of institutional discourses and policies. Whereas the object of his investigations often focuses on how institutions represent themselves through the production of documents and media, the intent in *Speaking Tours* was more oblique: to examine the lacunae and disruptions opened up by MUSEOPATHY's interventions. Robertson's working method was also differently grounded. Rather than working in isolation to develop an analysis, as is conventional for writers and artists, this dialogic performance personally engaged the intelligentsia of the art and academic communities. It thus foregrounded the network of social involvement essential to creative and intellectual activity as much as it gathered data about an exhibition and its locations.

The richness of interpretations emerging in Robertson's discussion tours revealed that artists and institutions retain only partial control over the intended meanings and experiences elicited by their objects, exhibitions and narratives. The juxtaposition of artworks and artifacts disturbed traditional methods of apprehending and understanding held to be appropriate to each genre of objects. Distinct from processes of "reading" a prescribed museum script, *Speaking Tours* engaged MUSEOPATHY as a social stage for the interactive framing of the exhibition as event.

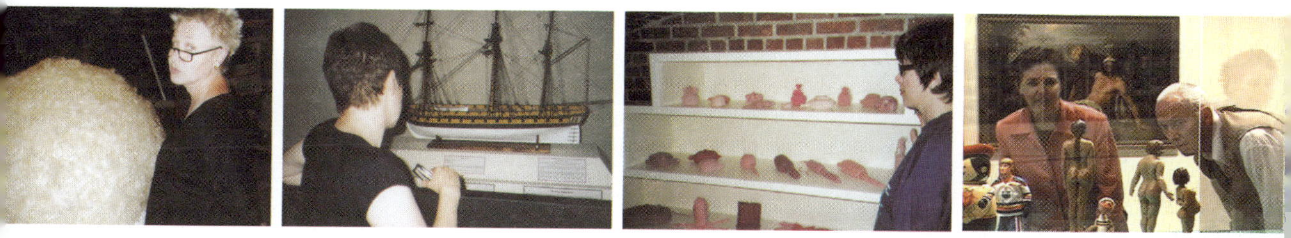

Clive Robertson, performance stills, *Speaking Tours* 2001

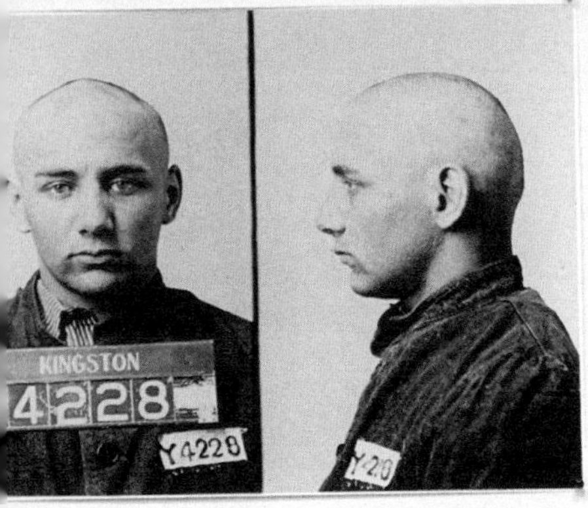
KINGSTON
4228
Y4228

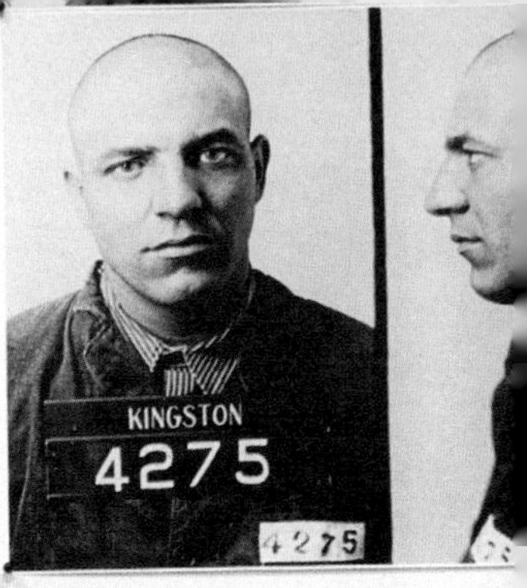
KINGSTON
4275
4275

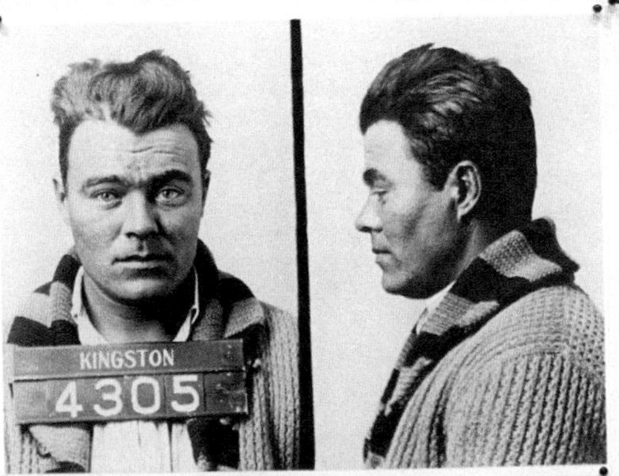
KINGSTON
4305

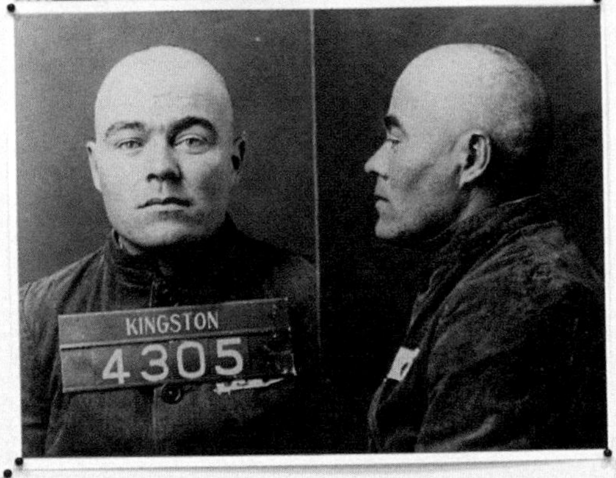
KINGSTON
4305

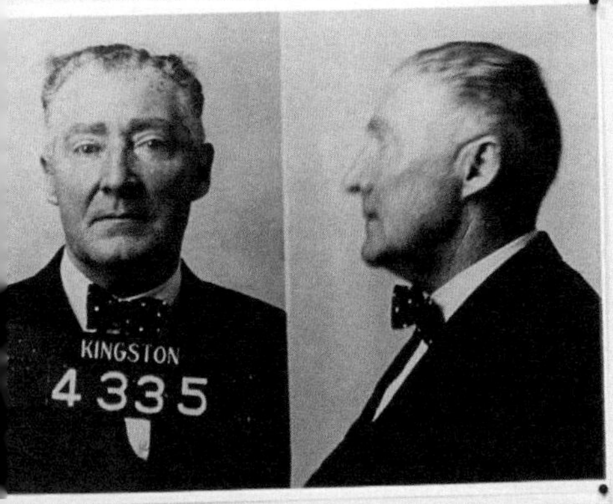
KINGSTON
4335

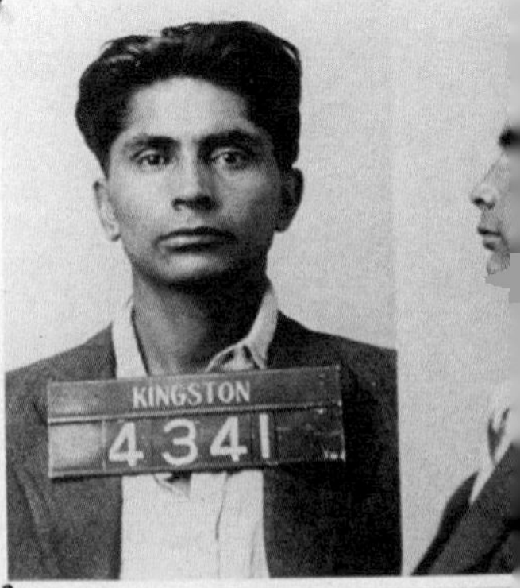
KINGSTON
4341

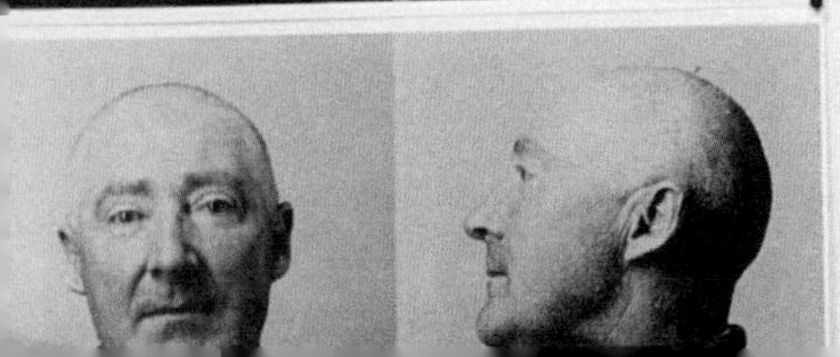

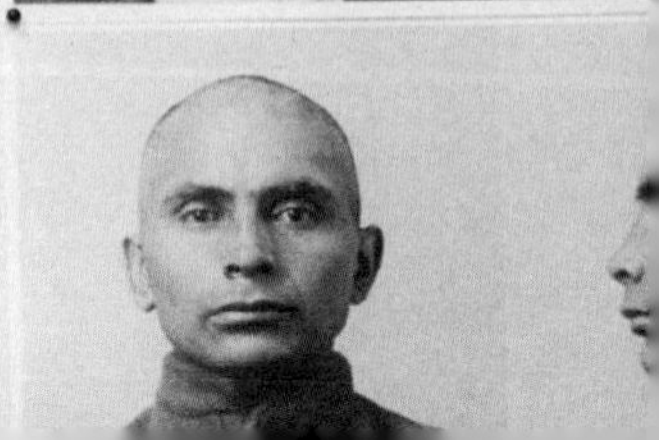

COLLECTIONEERING

Jim Drobnick and Jennifer Fisher

COLLECTIONEERING PRESENTED an integral counterpoint to the site-specific artists' installations and performances. Resulting from a two-year-long material trek through the vitrines and storerooms of a dozen Kingston museums and historical sites, we selected and placed over four hundred objects in a series of hybrid arrangements which mixed art and artifacts in ludic and discordant juxtapositions. It was no coincidence that the title of this exhibition calls to mind the activities of orienteering and mountaineering, pursuits that match physical endeavour with luck, patience, intuition and focus. The contemporary art spaces of the Agnes Etherington Art Centre sported a lively cross-section of the region's diverse and vital material heritage. On a civic level, it tracked how a culture collects itself and constructs an historical, geographic and public identity. On a museological level, it reconfigured conventional exhibition discourse and proposed a dialectical display practice.

TEMPTING PROVENANCE

WHILE MUSEUM ARTIFACTS ARE CUSTOMARILY obtained by the means of donation or purchase, many of the objects featured in COLLECTIONEERING entered their respective museums by highly uncommon means. Artifacts were acquired by being confiscated, abandoned, retired, rendered obsolete, salvaged, won in competition, lived with, excavated and surgically removed. Although situated in an art gallery, COLLECTIONEERING featured objects that were created, selected or found by

Detail, Constellation #16

individuals not usually associated with artistic production: prisoners and their guards; doctors, nurses and patients; sailors and boatbuilders; hockey players and coaches; university students and geologists; cadets and soldiers. Many objects derive from specialized collections that pioneered the accumulation of remarkable troves, as in the case of prison and medical paraphernalia.

Precise provenance of many of the extraordinary objects in COLLECTIONEERING was incomplete and unverifiable. Besides being gathered by professional curators in various fields, artifacts held in Kingston's museums also found their way into collections by chance and serendipity. At one extreme, objects arrived embellished with sensational or dramatic anecdotes, such as those handed down by adventurous world travellers and overseas military personnel. At the other extreme, objects appeared anonymously and unannounced. Divers and treasure hunters sometimes furtively (and one supposes remorsefully) dropped off boxes outside the Marine Museum's doors containing illegally scavenged goods from untraceable shipwrecks — unexpected presents known in-house as "the guilts." Still other objects carried little knowledge of the maker or specific context. Shivs and shanks, for instance, are among contraband items confiscated from prisoners so regularly that few, if any, records are kept. COLLECTIONEERING presented a number of items rescued from storeroom oblivion. Without definite provenance such objects become blank slates for the imagination to sketch-in and define. The temptation of unspecified heritage leaves these artifacts open to the projection of meanings and interpretations — and both the risk and poetry this activity implies.

MATERIAL CONSTELLATIONS

As an experiment in display prototypes, COLLECTIONEERING presented twenty-three material groupings — what we termed *constellations* — composed of objects of vastly different origins. Our exhibitionary constellations were a materialist version of Walter Benjamin's notion of a constellatory epistemology.[1] In the same way that a constellation is formed of numerous stars, the thematic concept of each display was the result of the gravitational force of its proximal artifacts. COLLECTIONEERING's clusters of objects signified in conjunctural ways. Each arrangement retained the integrity of the individual objects, yet at the same time revealed the polysemy that can result as the presence of other objects initiates and influences ideas. The meanings produced were not closed or absolute, but provisional and peripherally experienced. The relationships set up in these scenarios of engagement were

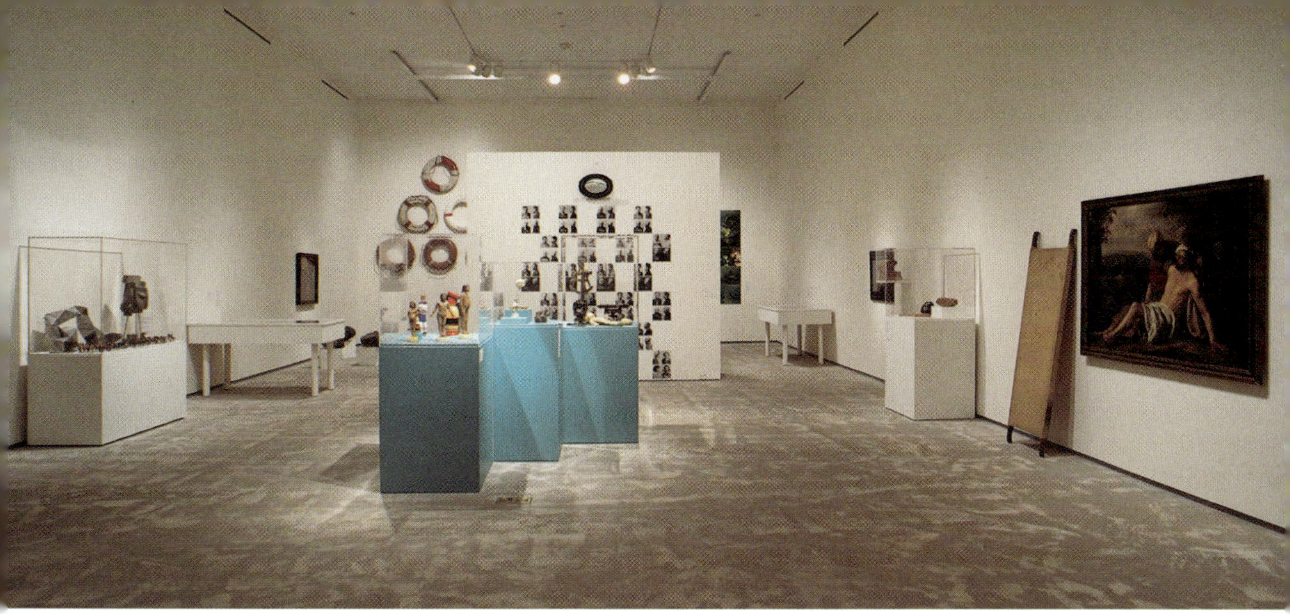

COLLECTIONEERING, installation view

semically open, like philosophical contemplations or Zen koans that elicit intense engagement but defy singular, concrete interpretations.

It was important to us that an ethics of equivalence was maintained between museum genres. Art was considered on the same level as other forms of material culture. Precedence was given to neither art nor history, beauty nor provenance, craftsmanship nor uniqueness. As art objects gained new meanings by being placed alongside artifacts, everyday and atypical objects were reframed in terms of aesthetic experience. This non-hierarchical display strategy deliberately foregrounded a mutuality between objects of dissimilar discursive formations, as distinct from exhibitions which position and evaluate objects within monological disciplines. Staged with neither interpretative texts nor governing thematic narratives, the objects in the exhibition encompassed both the strengths and anomalies of the eight host collections. Labels, however, identified the lending museum for each object and served as an essential thread to the originating disciplinary context, even as it was being dramatically rearticulated. While artifacts are sanctioned as evidence of disciplinary "truths" (of authenticity, excellence, rarity), the constellations of COLLECTIONEERING sustained the contradictions that such discourses, at times, contain or gloss over. Yet any sense of irreverence in our acts of recontextualization was not oriented to the objects themselves, but rather towards unsettling exhibition conventions that confine multivalent objects within authoritative habits and singular truths.

RHETORICS OF ARRANGEMENT

As forms of rhetoric — or persuasive communication — exhibitions provide convincing presentations of material culture through continuums marked by text, whether in the form of printed labels, interpretative panels or audio-guide scripts. But in another sense, exhibitions impel beholders to actually *enact* particular identifications. In theorizing exhibition rhetorics, Stephen Bann translates forms of textual rhetoric — metonymy and synecdoche — into the spatial terms of exhibition. Metonymic displays, he writes, pose objects as specimens dislocated from their originating discourse; an over-arching display framework then imposes classification and significance. The practice of inserting non-art objects into an aesthetic milieu, thus making them "art," then, can be understood in terms of a metonymic impulse (e.g., Duchamp's readymades). Synecdochic displays, in turn, consider objects as relics, as fragments of a whole which, like puzzle pieces, fit together to form a greater reconstituted totality. This approach is evident in period rooms or living history museums — such as Bellevue House — which attempt to recreate the entire ambiance of a specific period or place.[2]

The constellations of COLLECTIONEERING shared some aspects of metonymy and synecdoche, but in general their repositioning of objects involved neither a new, cogent classificatory scheme nor a larger, illusionistic *mise-en-scène*. Resisting such totalities, COLLECTIONEERING's constellatory arrangements shared more with the partiality of assemblage, as well as with other rhetorical strategies, such as irony (dual or contradictory meaning), or syntactical ploys usually considered faults or errors, such as catachresis (misapplication of words, i.e., mixed metaphors) and malapropism (inappropriate use of words). By carefully cultivating overdeterminations and deliberate disjunctures of genre, historical era and typology, the object arrangements generated double and triple meanings.[3] The improper (and sometimes impertinent) display techniques used in COLLECTIONEERING yielded irresolvable contradictions, humorous and poignant contrasts, aesthetic and politicized readings, all contingently and provisionally uttered within the display forum of a temporary exhibition.

By juxtaposing curiosities and masterpieces, trophies and specimens, fetishes and contraband, COLLECTIONEERING created awry associations between incompatible objects, emphasizing alternative ways of ruminating upon their artful and auratic capacities. No authoritative interpretations or systematic narratives were presented; no titles were given to the groupings; what remained was a provocative heterogeneity in which diverse meanings resonated and were conspicuously open to audience negotiation. Rather than closure, we sought to construct constellations that were charged with specific intensities that would invite engagements which encompassed poetic, idiosyncratic, critical and interdisciplinary acts of reflection.

THE POSTMODERN *WUNDERKAMMER*

The idiosyncratic arrangements central to COLLECTIONEERING were continuous with those of a syncretic form of premodern display — the *wunderkammer* or "cabinet of curiosities." Traditional *wunderkammern* from the sixteenth to the eighteenth centuries included artisanal objects, relics, travel souvenirs and wondrous items of natural history, all drawn together by the passionate whims of their collectors. Access to these collections was limited to the intimate circles of the owner and involved a sensorially rich viewing experience. Each object was a touchstone for tales of acquisition and significance. As such, the *wunderkammer* created a juncture of empirical objects and eccentric theologies as highly personalized readings of reality.[4]

Despite the eclipse of the *wunderkammer* by the professionalization of collecting and the institutionalization of museums in the late eighteenth and early nineteenth centuries, the cabinet of curiosity remains an unruly exhibition type embodying much of what linear, didactic, instrumental presentations seek to control. The *wunderkammer*, in essence, represents the dark remnants of irrationality cast aside and repressed by the project of the Enlightenment. What is fascinating about the *wunderkammer* as a display form is that it resists taxonomic mastery, eludes logical explanation, bears hybridized identities, and inspires reverie, and so resists the limits of categorizing imperatives.

Any project reviving a premodern display prototype in the postmodern era carries with it certain risks. If "curiosity" was the overriding sentiment pertaining to the collection and appreciation of the original *wunderkammer*, what purposes can it serve in the contemporary realm when science has purportedly explained many of life's mysteries? What might it mean to pose COLLECTIONEERING as a "postmodern *wunderkammer*"? The objects chosen by us during our months of curatorial flânerie extended the etymological root shared by both "curate" and "curious." Admittedly, our curiosity was a governing impulse as we found ourselves drawn to intriguing objects. To some extent our personal proclivities and recognitions formed the trajectory of assimilation and arrangement that deliberately blurred disciplines, genres and styles. Our stance was self-conscious in selecting and juxtaposing artifacts.

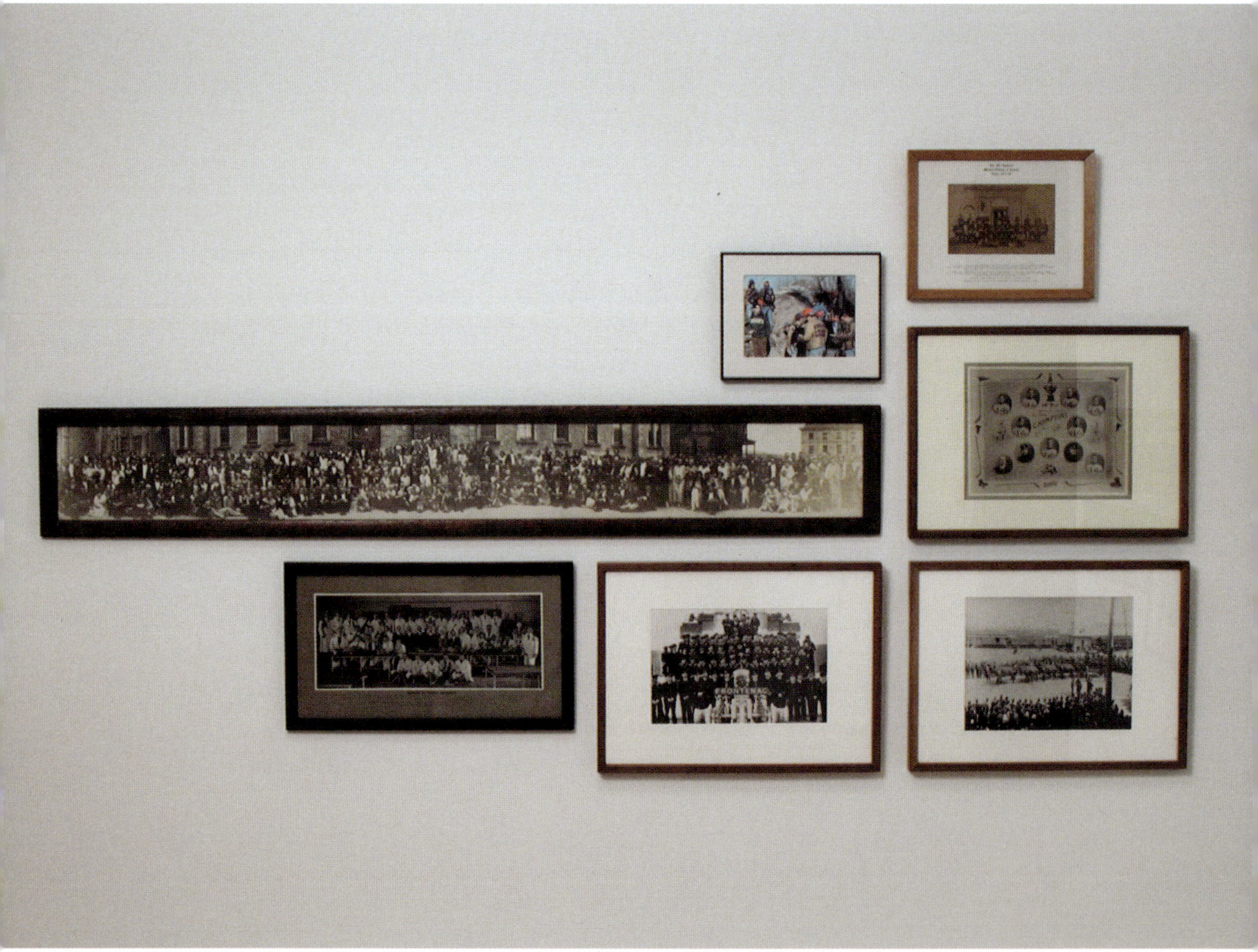

Constellation #1

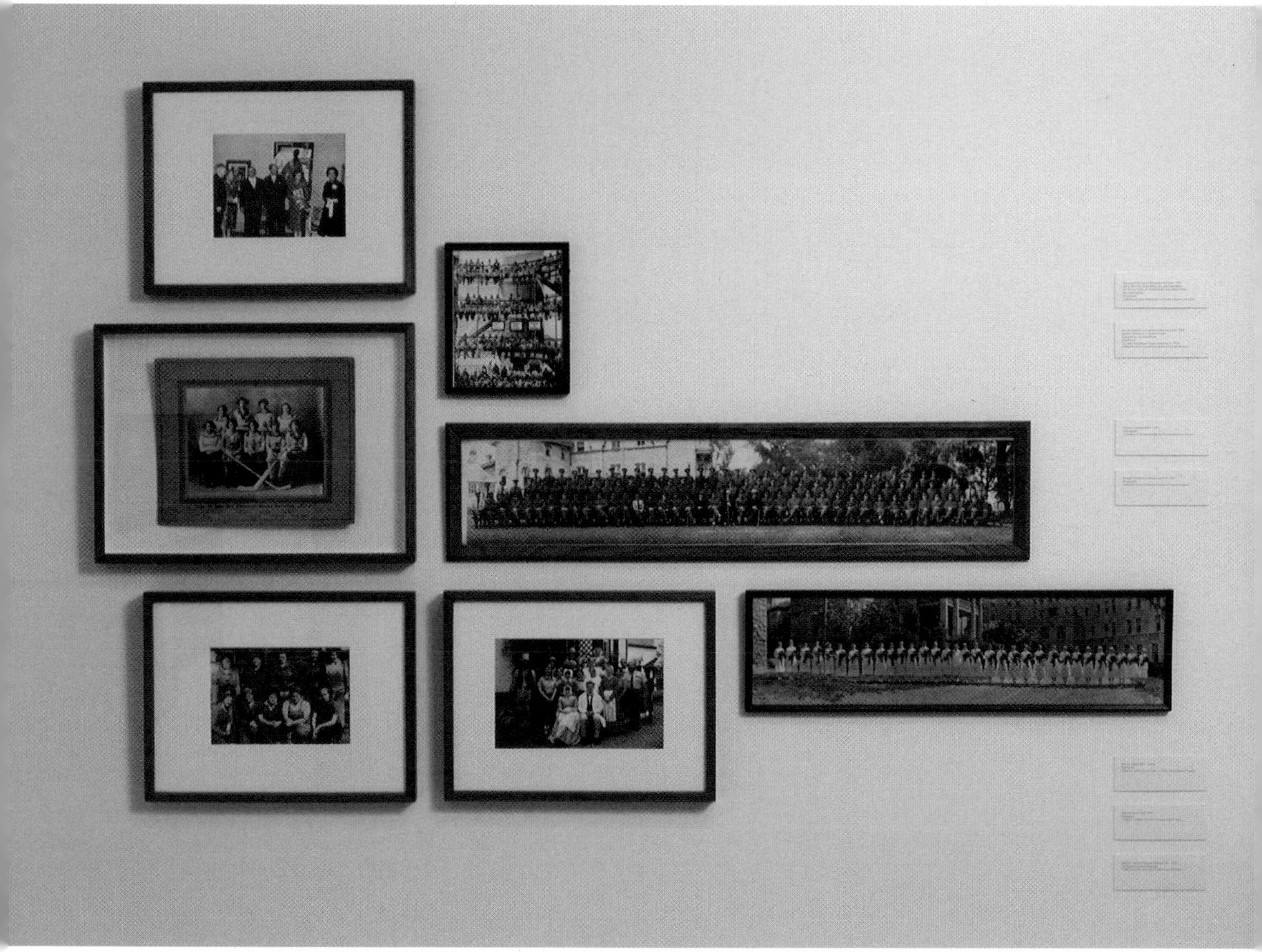

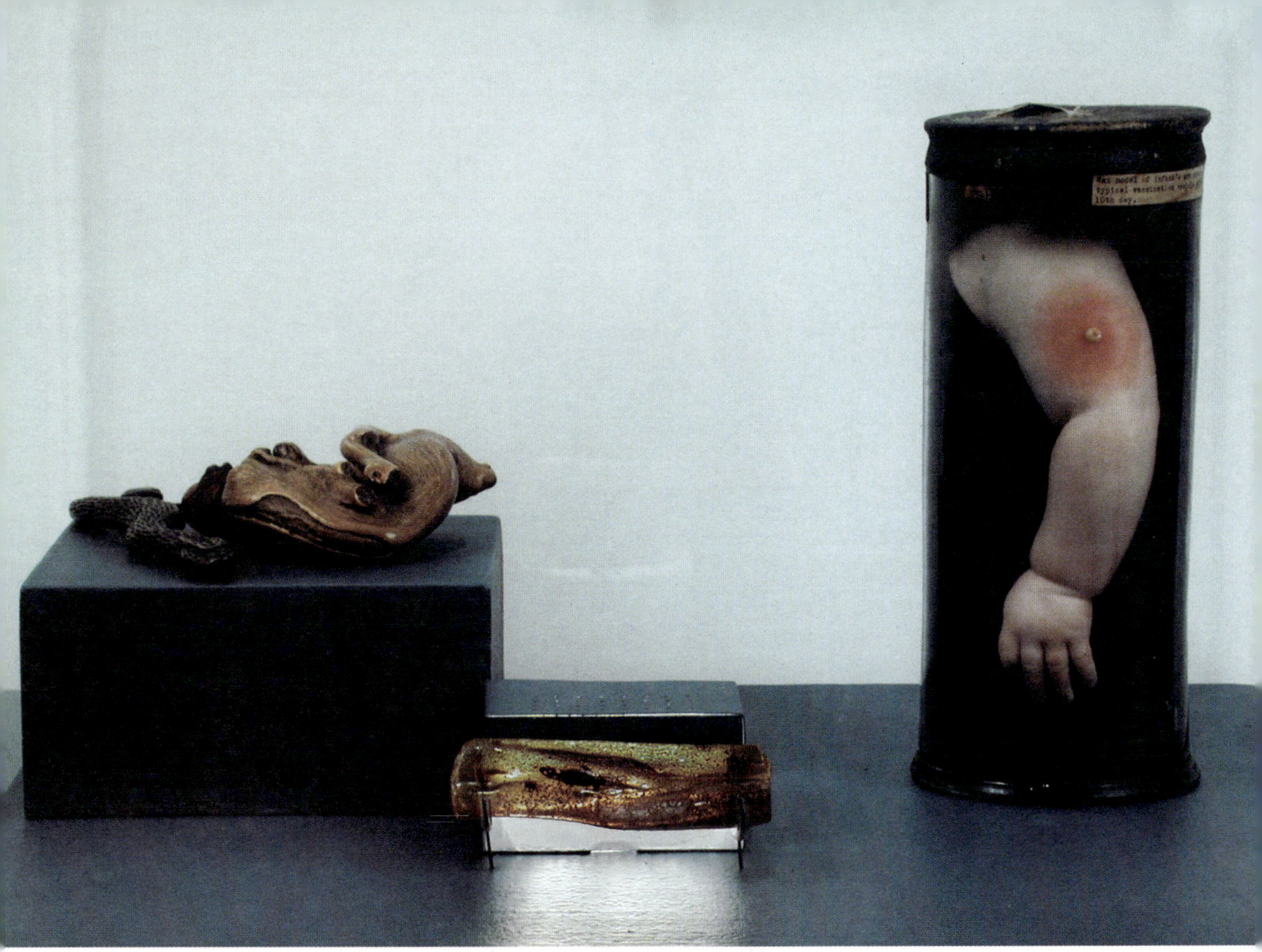

Constellation #21

Rather than assuming to represent a personal world through a transcendent meta-collection, COLLECTIONEERING re-articulated the significance of objects contiguous to their collections, in a sense creating an *intra-collection* that linked objects within the exhibitionary complex of Kingston. While COLLECTIONEERING retained the textual conventions of exhibition rhetoric, the constellation display typology — in continuity with installation-based art works — explicitly emphasized the extra-discursive aspects of exhibitions: their experiential and affective impact.

To enter COLLECTIONEERING, beholders passed one of two "glossary murals" — walls of words hinting at the numerous ways "objects" can be defined, evaluated and codified: as artifact, collectible, evidence, fetish, masterpiece, or tchotchke, to name just a few. This deliberately non-expository compendium suggested a galaxy of valencies that result when objects from vastly divergent governing discourses are merged.

COLLECTIONEERING's constellations can be roughly grouped into four display typologies: arrangements based on the *wunderkammer*, and those that were dialectical, indexical and humanist. In regard to the first type, several constellations directly referenced the classic *wunderkammer* and its two main affective volitions: enigma and idiosyncrasy. The enigmatic constellations featured objects that problematically confused categories (evaporating distinctions between human, animal, botanical, and mineral) and created uncanny connections (between beauty and grotesqueness, banality and mystery). Such "unstable" artifacts were collected together in one arrangement of "emergent objects" (#21), things immersed in, or erupting from, something else — such as a lizard fossilized in amber, a face appearing in a tobacco case fashioned out of a tree knot, an inflamed smallpox pustule on a wax model of a baby's arm, and eerie underwater photographs of shipwrecks. These items exist in a precarious stasis, as if caught in the midst of apparent but unfinished metamorphosis, unstably arrested in states of becoming or decomposition.

The idiosyncratic juxtapositions placed disparate objects into amalgamations so "stretched" that attempts to rationalize them could only rest upon notions of playfulness, lyricism, humour, or self-conscious contrivance. A chamois practice baby, used to rehearse delivery room procedures, was the centrepiece of an explicitly idiosyncratic intersection of medical, military and marine navigational aids (#15). Surrounded by a theodolite, sextant and telescope, the E.T.-like post-partum model (with placenta) suggested an alien meeting of the technological and the human. Here ships and fetuses bore associational and geographic similarities: both manoeuvre through fluid media and, historically, in Kingston, the launch of a ship and hospital birthing procedures occurred within a few hundred metres of each other.[5]

The second constellation type was premised upon the strategy of *dialectical arrangements*. Objects of diverse origins abut and dynamically play off each other to create internal tensions and stressed meanings. These juxtapositions unleashed a third level of display-signification through their proxemic associations which challenged conventionally held meanings, assumptions and interpretations of the individual objects. These constellations tended to raise political questions regarding class difference, the power of institutions and industries, or the constructions of history.

One dialectical arrangement contrasted items designed to penetrate the human body — to either injure or save a life (#18). Shivs (prisoners' weapons), surgical tools and an Ashanti executioner's knife signalled extreme differences in technological sophistication and artisanal skill. Despite the differences between a dagger created

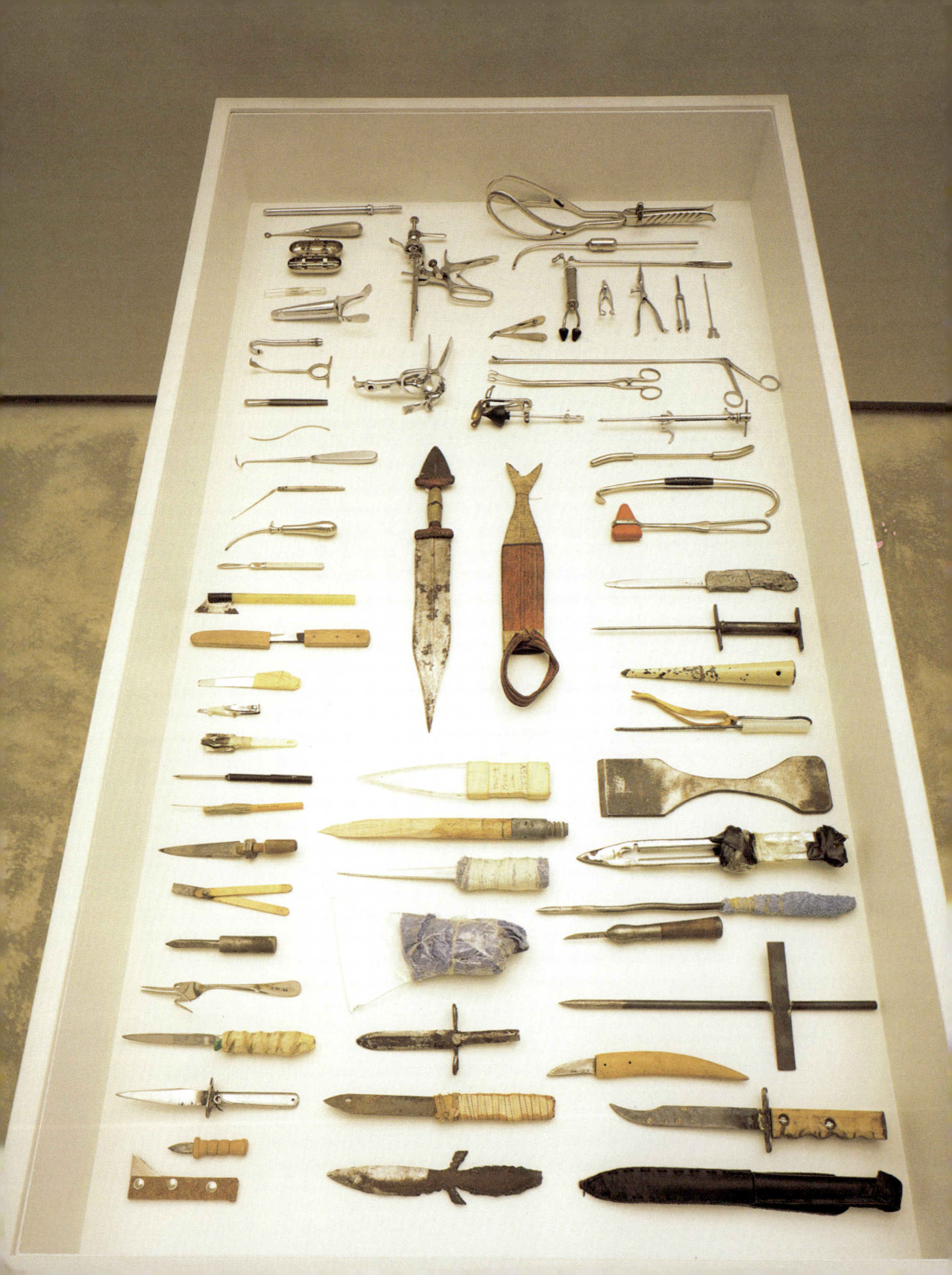

from a razor blade and toothbrush, an intricately decorated ritual blade and fishskin sheath, or an ergonomic stainless steel scalpel, each revealed remarkable ingenuity. This posing of artifacts evoked comparisons between sanctioned and unsanctioned violence, whether through the lethal inventiveness of inmates, the visceral intensity of medical procedures, or lawful technologies of capital punishment.

Another dialectical constellation juxtaposed a plaster cast of a mythological bust with seven fake heads confiscated from prisoners' cells (#7). Both the sculpture and the escape heads suggested a kind of bravado occurring at polarities of the class divide. The oversized Hellenic bust, representing the pinnacle of classical civilization, hovered above crude bricolaged decoys. While the studio cast was oriented to education, the prisoners' heads were geared to deception. Yet these contrary uses of portraiture divulged similarities regardless of the apparent polarity of aesthetic beauty and desperate functionality — art is often utilized as a form of escape, and inmates can gain renown as "escape artists."[6]

COLLECTIONEERING hosted a number of painting-object constellations that explored the ramifications of matching thematic representations with indexical traces. The relationship of artworks with "real" objects brought together the metaphorical with the literal, the iconic with things that had been used, some over many years. In this third display type, which we termed *indexical allegories*, a mutual transference occurred between objects of the constellation: artifacts gained semiological and auratic power, while representations gained grounding in tangible lives and events.

One indexical allegory positioned *Jacob's Dream* (c. 1700), attributed to Paolo de Matteis, against five ropes and ladders confiscated from inmates, as well as a prisoner's acrylic painting (#8). Signed F.T.W. (prison vernacular for "Fuck The World") Towers, its composition of a sunset and grotto was strikingly similar to the Baroque painting, with the exception of an additional element — two Satan's Choice choppers. The biblical story of Jacob's reverie, a ladder that would deliver him to heaven and away from life's afflictions, when refracted through actual escape devices fabricated by prisoners (among them is Tyrone Conn's infamous ladder[7]) attested to the compelling interlinkages between emancipatory fantasies in both the physical and spiritual domains.

A second example of indexical allegory paired the painting *The Good Samaritan* (1640), attributed to Lambert Jacobz, with a medical stretcher believed to have been used during the First World War (#10). While the oil on canvas depicted the virtuous act of caring for a vulnerable stranger, the canvas stretcher displayed the actual

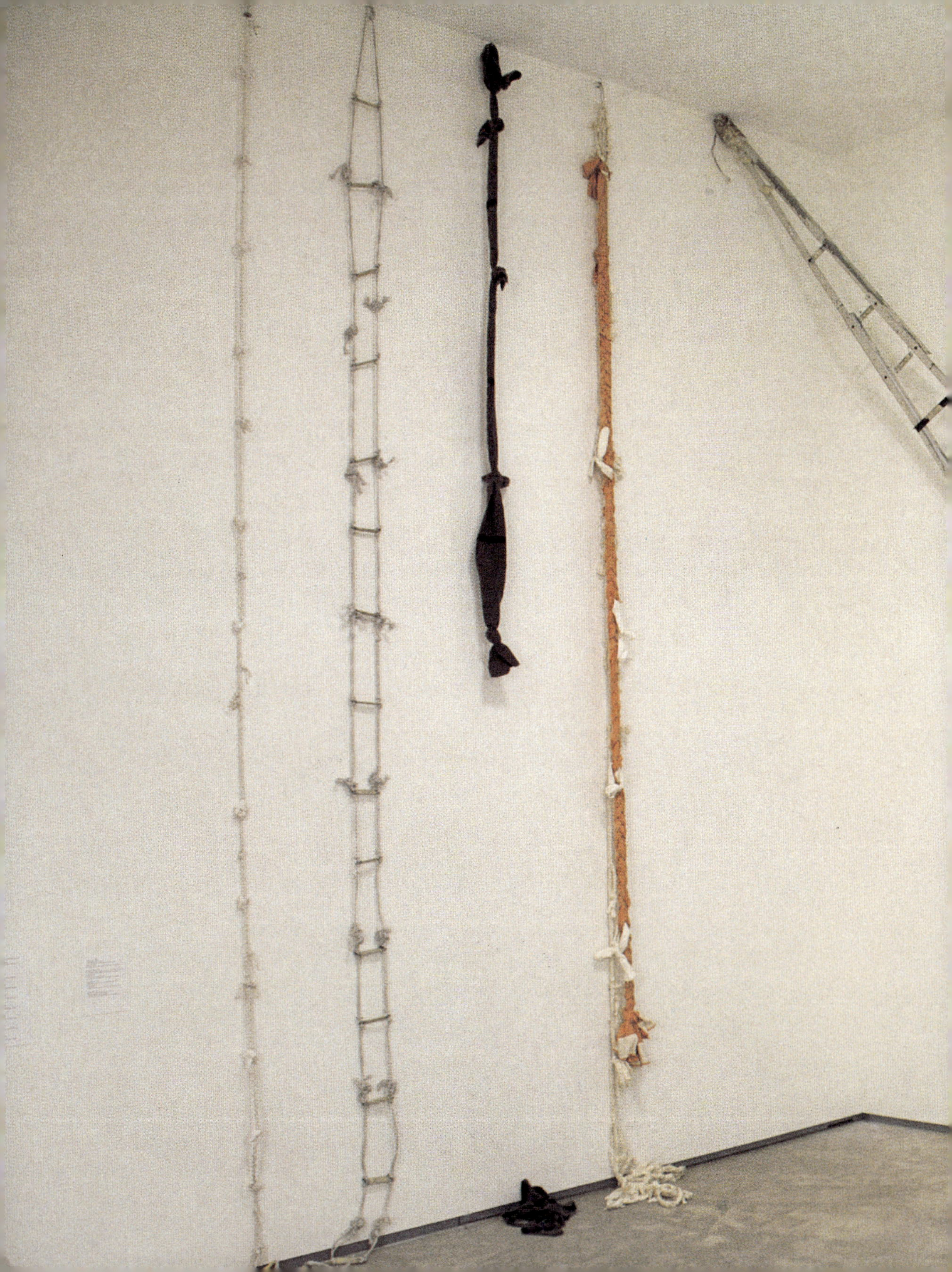

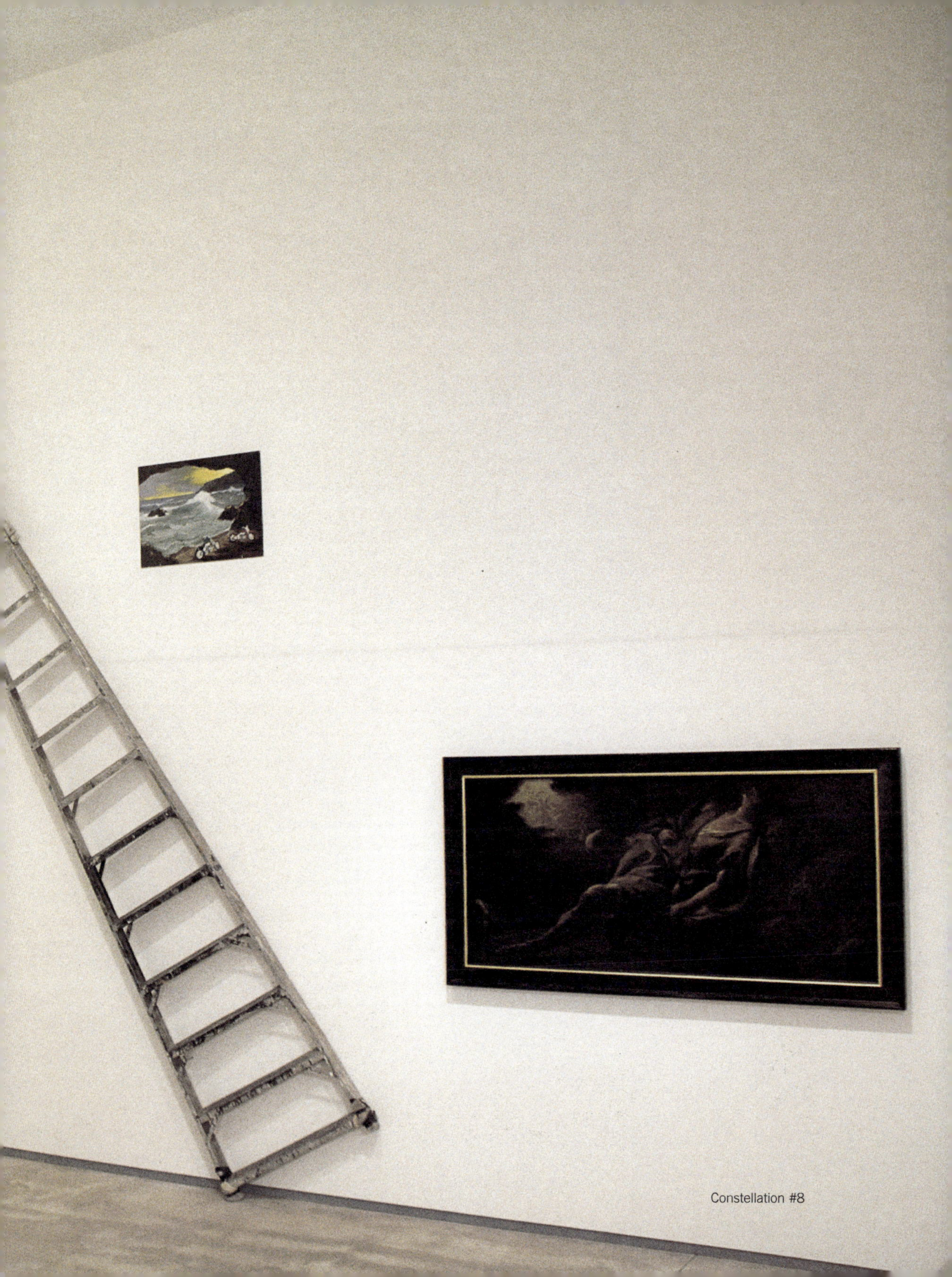

Constellation #8

stains of injured bodies and its wooden handles the patina of many assisting hands. The dark horror and inclement conditions of twentieth-century rescue efforts became another site in which the symbol of compassion conveyed in the biblical parable was literally exemplified.[8]

The fourth display type centred upon values traditionally presumed to be shared by human beings regardless of time, geography or social situation. These *humanistic constellations* expressed through their productive diversity of representation and fabrication gripping commonalities despite the diverse cultural formations of their makers. Rather than ascribing to some version of universalism, this curatorial rationale was concerned with interrogating how similarity and difference can be posed and negotiated in the artifactual domain.

In one constellation, a range of shields (Persian, Zulu, Australian Aboriginal, and one produced by Kingston Penitentiary inmates) and other defence technologies showed that behind the diversity of cultures, styles, craftsmanship and intended purposes lay a preoccupation with protection as a common end (#3). Presenting items selected from nearly every MUSEOPATHY site, from prisoners' armour to hockey pads, from lead nipple shields to preparator's gloves, the concern with aegis — militarily and otherwise — is a predominant theme in Kingston area museums.

Left to right: Constellations #2, 3, 4, 5

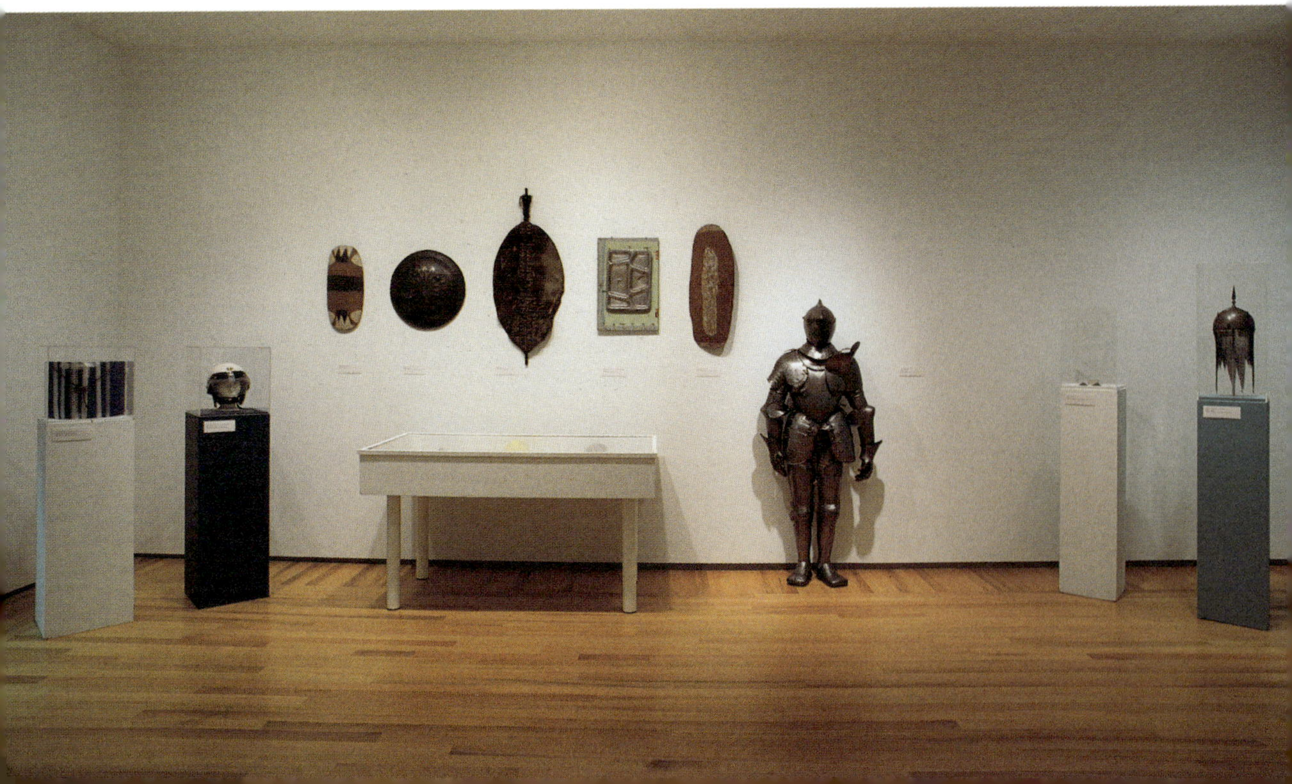

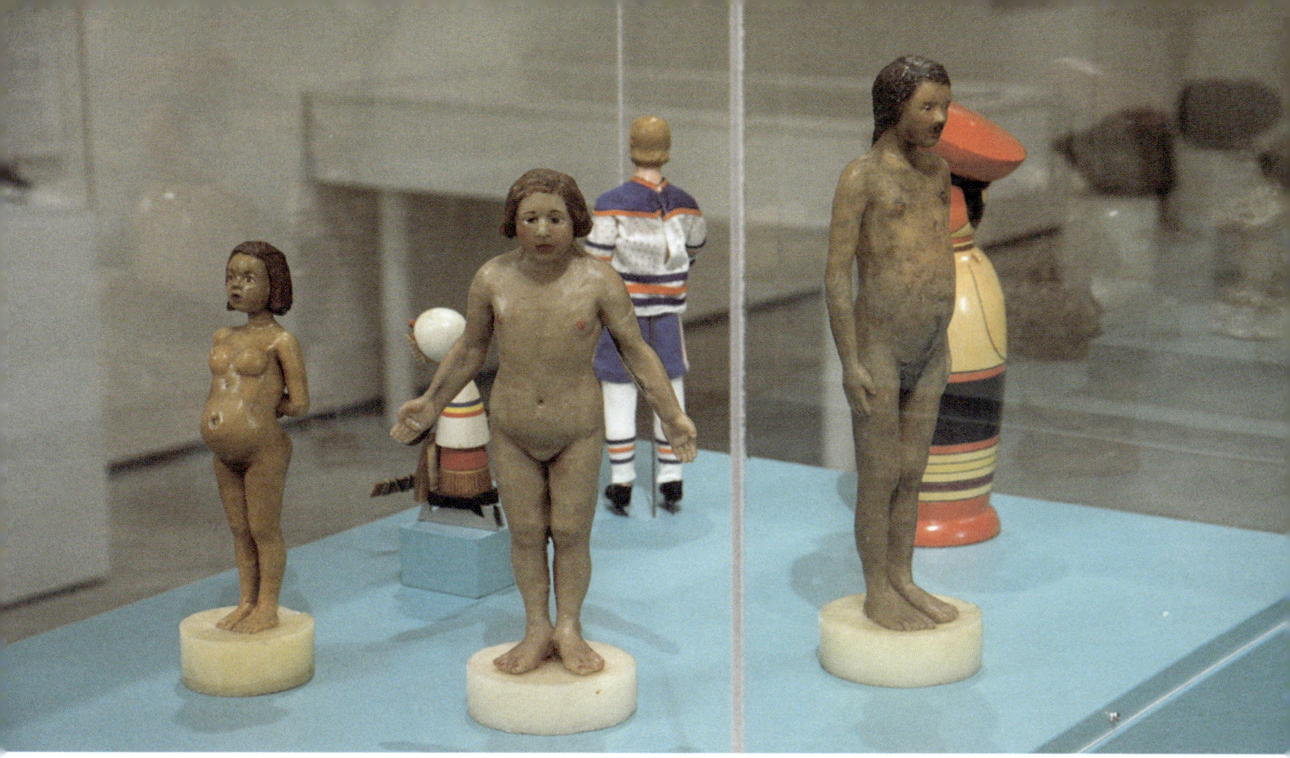

Constellation #13

Another humanistic constellation featured miniature figures that render the body symbolically controllable (#13). Contrasting modes of corporeal figuration in popular, artistic and professional cultures reflected the variety of ends such representations mobilize. One display case grouped wax medical somatotypes — models of female physiological pathologies — with hockey dolls from Russia, Romania and Canada. The dissimilarity of nude wax figures (sculpted by Marjorie Winslow in the 1940s[9]), sport memorabilia, and a Wayne Gretzky doll evoked compellingly different affects. Together they demonstrated the distinctions between skilled artisanship, mass merchandising and folkloric production in human representations of analogous scale.[10]

Whether exhibiting wondrous, dialectical, indexical or humanistic display typologies, the curatorial act of creating the constellations of COLLECTIONEERING was potentially perilous. Arranging objects in unusual combinations, asking audiences to interpret oblique connections, as well as blurring the distinction between curatorial and artistic activity, all defied normative "ways of reading" embedded in traditional museum display practices. COLLECTIONEERING asked beholders to engage in a cognitive process of making connections, and thus contribute their own perceptions to the objects and constellations.

NOTES

1. Walter Benjamin, *The Origin of German Tragic Drama*, London: NLB, 1977, pp. 34–35.

2. Stephen Bann, *The Clothing of Clio: A Study of the Representation of History in Nineteenth-Century Britain and France*, Cambridge, UK: Cambridge University Press, 1984.

3. Anachrony and incongruity have long formed the basic logics of montage, collage, and assemblage. Two watershed museum interventions likewise operate via underacknowledged tropes. Fred Wilson discusses his *Mining the Museum* (1994) in terms of "mixed metaphors," and Joseph Kosuth's *Play of the Unmentionable* (1992) utilizes ironic contrasts between text and art to deconstruct the supposed verities espoused by art's censors over the past several centuries.

4. Stephen Bann, "Shrines, Curiosities, and the Rhetoric of Display," *Visual Display: Culture Beyond Appearances*, eds. Lynne Cooke and Peter Wollen, New York and Seattle: DIA and Bay Press, 1995, p. 24.

5. Three other *wunderkammer*-type constellations were presented. One displayed mysterious objects (medical, geological, biological and cultural anomalies) (#11). A second staged a contest between two sculptures and toy soldiers arranged in formations of attacking and defending modern art (#17). A third — pacemakers and life rings — featured life preservers that either surround or are implanted into the body (#20).

6. Another dialectical constellation contrasted poisons and remedies — and their shifting legal status — in the form of patent medicines, pharmaceuticals, contraband drugs and other substances (#22). A fourth arrangement featured inmate admission photographs juxtaposed with a convex mirror (#16). As viewers contemplated the extreme transformation of the "before and after" images, their own reflection in the mirror was inverted — an allusion to how dramatically one's social standing can be reconfigured.

7. On the night of May 7, 1999, Tyrone Conn escaped Kingston Penitentiary, the first over-the-wall escape in 41 years. Conn had assembled a ladder and an extension from shelving materials in the prison's industrial shop. The escape gained national attention. He was located in Toronto and died at his own hand before being apprehended.

8. Four other constellations utilized the AEAC's noteworthy Baroque paintings from the collection of Drs. Alfred and Isabel Bader. *Ecce Homo*, attributed to Anthony Van Dyck, was framed by poison-tipped arrows from Papua New Guinea, thus collapsing the museal distinctions of "masterpieces" and "artifacts" (#23). Other painting/object juxtapositions demonstrated a continuity of interests across time and geography. Nicolaes Verkolje's *Susanna and the Elders* was set against an inmate-manufactured jewelry box decoupaged with nude figures (#12). Despite the differences between biblical inspiration and pornography, formal and carnal resonances bridged the gap separating these two "cabinet pictures." Other pairings were based on responses to actions and items in the paintings. In front of Jacob Pynas's *The Stoning of St. Stephen*, specimens of metamorphic, volcanic and glaciated rocks teasingly challenged spectators to join in the mayhem and reflect on how landscape can be used as a weapon (#19). The nineteenth-century key to the doors of the Kingston Penitentiary was aligned to a similar key in a painting of St. Peter, contrasting the notions of gatekeeping in both physical and otherworldly realms (#9).

9. Marjorie Winslow was a Kingston sculptor commissioned by Dr. Edwin Robertson, chairman of the Department of Obstetrics and Gynecology at Queen's University, to sculpt obstetric models, gynecologic pathologies and miniature representations of female somatotypes. She used moulage, a wax casting technique originating in the eighteenth century and utilizing beeswax, talc and oil paint. Her anatomical specimens are reportedly one of the last major groups of medical moulages to be produced in the world. See Fiona Mattatall and Rona Rustige, "A Very Real Art," *Canadian Medical Association Journal*, April 3, 2001, pp. 1027–1028.

10. Other humanist constellations included a series of group photographs of the communities associated with each MUSEOPATHY site (#1), a vitrine contemplating the infant in medical, artistic and popular cultures (#14), and a display that pivoted around threshold moments in the lives of notable individuals in Canadian history (#6).

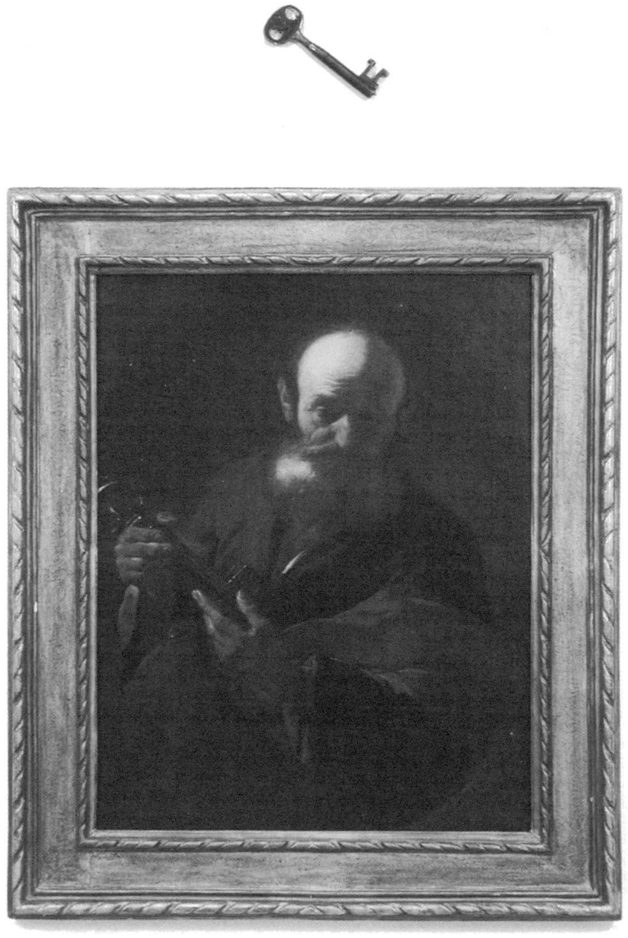

Constellation #9

COLLECTIONEERING

The artworks and artifacts comprising COLLECTIONEERING are listed below in groups to convey their constellatory arrangement in the exhibition.

KEY

AE	Agnes Etherington Art Centre
BH	Bellevue House National Historic Site
CSC	Correctional Service of Canada Museum
IH	International Ice Hockey Federation Museum
MG	Miller Museum of Geology and Mineralogy
MHC	Museum of Health Care at Kingston
MM	Marine Museum of the Great Lakes at Kingston
MT	Murney Tower National Historic Site
RMC	Royal Military College of Canada Museum

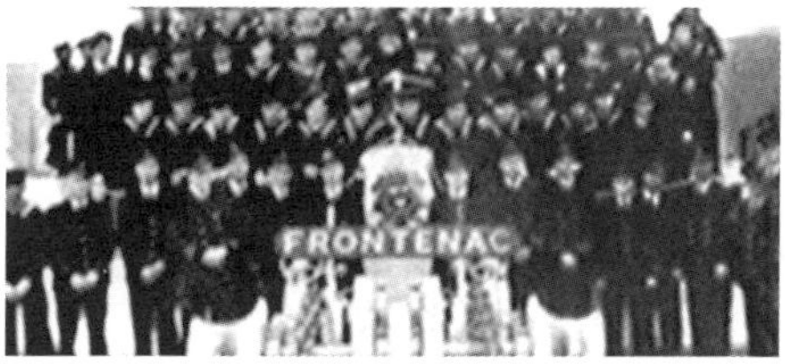

1

Sailors from the *Frontenac*, 1900s
photograph (MM)

Bellevue House Staff, 1995
photograph (BH)

Geology Students on a Field Trip, c. 1995
digital print (MG)

Graduation Ball "Morning After," 1923
photograph (RMC)

Inmate Audience in Kingston Penitentiary Dome, 1955
digital print (BH)

Kingston General Hospital Nursing Graduating Class, 1939
photograph (MHC)

Kingston Intermediate OHA Hockey Team, 1925
photograph (IH)

Kingston Penitentiary Guards and Staff, 1937
photograph (CSC)

"Old Eighteen" Cadets, c. 1878
photograph (RMC)

Opening of the Agnes Etherington Art Centre, 1957
photograph (AE)

Queen's Medicine Graduating Class, 1923
photograph (MHC, GIFT OF DR. BRACKEN)

Sir John A. Macdonald Funeral Procession, 1891
photograph (BH)

Women Shipbuilders, 1940s
photograph (MM)

Women's Hockey Team, 1923
photograph (IH)

2

Inmate Body Armour, 2000
three-ring binder covers and masking tape (CSC)

Kingston Penitentiary Institutional Emergency Response Team Helmet, 1976
plastic, leather, foam, metal and adhesive letters (CSC)

3

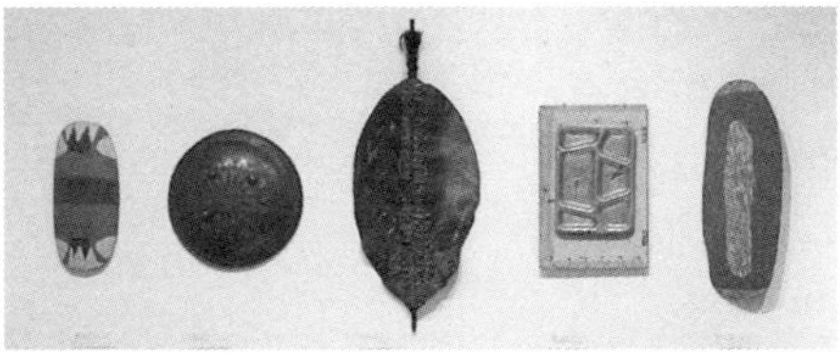

Shield (Australia, Central Queensland), n.d.
wood, paint and cloth (AE)

Shield (Persian), late seventeenth to early eighteenth century
steel (RMC, DOUGLAS COLLECTION)

Zulu Shield, n.d.
cowhide, wood and animal hair (RMC)

Inmate Shield, 1971
metal lunchtray and reclaimed wood (CSC)

Shield (Australian), n.d.
wood and paint (AE)

4

Hard Hat, 2001
plastic (MG)

Radiology Safety Goggles, 1940–1960
plastic and elastic (MHC, GIFT OF KGH RADIOLOGY DEPARTMENT)

Respirator (Canadian), 1940
mask and canister (RMC, ISSUED TO LT., LATER COL., C.F. WAY)

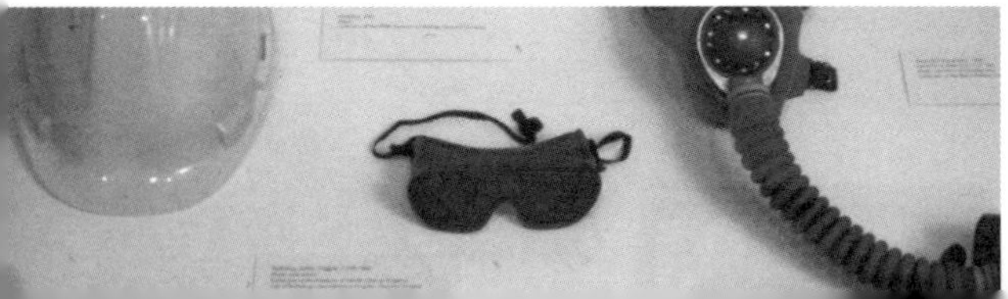

Combat Helmet (Canadian), c. 1939
steel
(RMC, WORN BY LT., LATER COL., C.F. WAY)

Gordie Bell Mask (Belleville McFarlands), c. 1960
moulded plastic (IH)

Knee and Leg Pads, c. 1960
plastic, leather and felt (IH)

Preparator's Gloves, 2001
cotton (AE)

Suit of Armour (Italian), sixteenth century
metal (RMC, DOUGLAS COLLECTION)

5

Kulah Khud Helmet (Persian), nineteenth century
metal (RMC, DOUGLAS COLLECTION)

Nipple Shields, late nineteenth century
lead (MHC, ANDERSON COLLECTION)

6

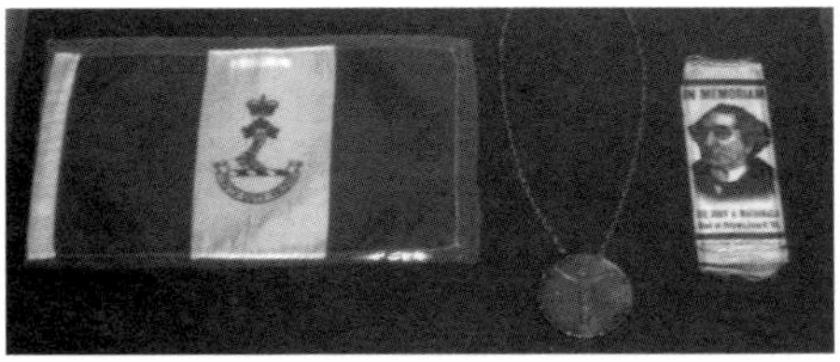

Flag Flown Aboard Space Shuttle *Atlantis*, 1995
(RMC, GIFT OF LT. COL. CHRIS HADFIELD)

Olympic Gold Medal, Ice Hockey, 1924
(IH, GIFT OF JACK CAMERON)

Sir John A. Macdonald Funeral Commemorative Ribbon, 1891
silk (BH, GIFT OF MRS. W. E. WILSON)

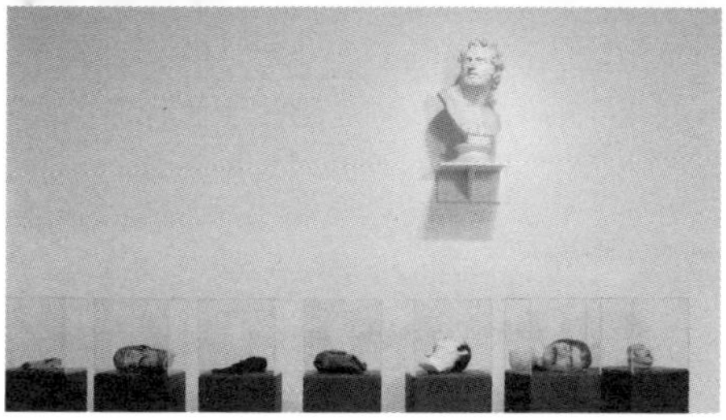

7

Inmate Decoy Heads, 1950s–1970s
mixed media, including newspaper, plaster, paint, hair, velour, felt, cardboard, toilet paper, mop, masking tape, rawhide (CSC)

Classical Bust Portrait,
nineteenth century
plaster (AE)

8

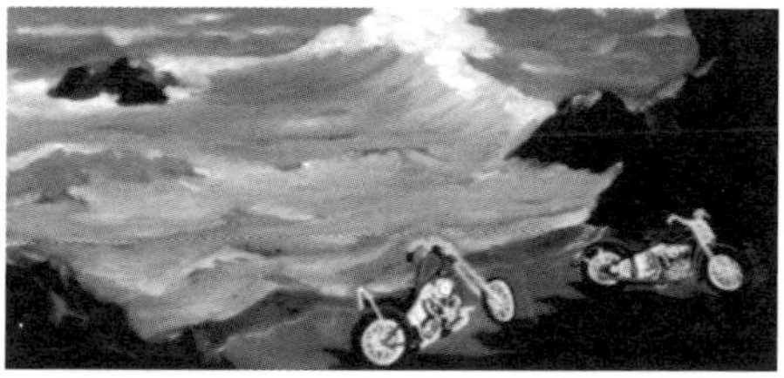

"FTW Towers"
Untitled, c. 1985
oil on canvas board (CSC)

Paolo de Matteis, attributed to
(Italian, 1662–1728)
Jacob's Dream, c. 1700
oil on canvas (AE, GIFT OF DRS. ALFRED AND ISABEL BADER, 1988)

Escape Ropes, 1970s
mixed media, including nylon cords, bed sheets, leather, coat hanger, hose clamps, wool blankets, curtains, grappling hooks (CSC)

Tyrone Conn
Escape Ladder, 1999
aluminum shop ladder, shelf supports, metal handles and draw-cords (CSC)

9

Kingston Penitentiary Main Gate Key,
nineteenth century
metal (CSC)

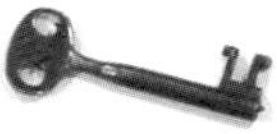

Anonymous (Italian)
St. Peter, seventeenth century
oil on canvas (AE, GIFT OF DRS. ALFRED AND ISABEL BADER, 1988)

10

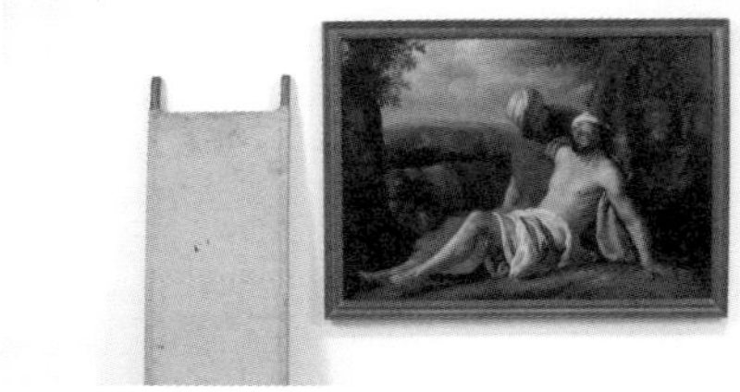

Stretcher, 1890s
canvas and wood (MHC, BIRD COLLECTION)

Lambert Jacobsz, attributed to (Dutch, c. 1598–1636)
The Good Samaritan, c. 1635
oil on canvas (AE, GIFT OF DRS. ALFRED AND ISABEL BADER, 1988)

11

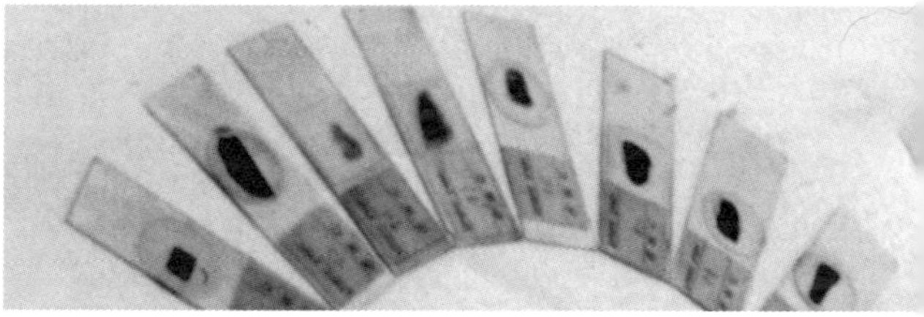

Histological Slides, 1920s
wood, glass and biological specimens
(MHC, BRACKEN COLLECTION)

Elephant Tooth, 1905
(RMC, COLLECTED BY RMC #45
COL. E.T. TAYLOR)

Hematite ("Kidney Ore")
Cumberland, England (MG)

Necklace (Papua New Guinea),
late nineteenth century
human teeth, shell beads and fibre cord (AE)

12

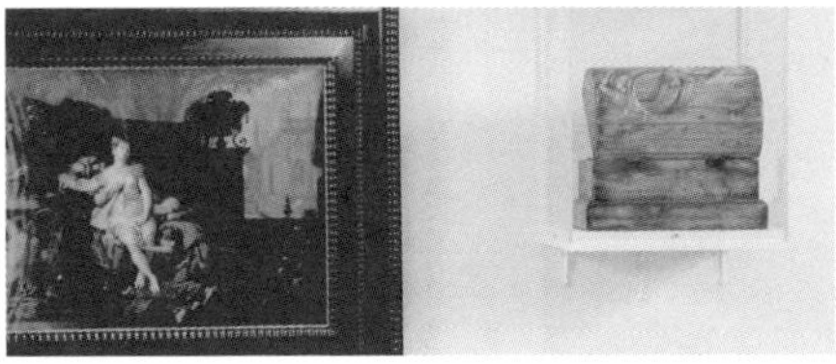

Nicolaes Verkolje (Dutch, 1673–1746)
Susanna and the Elders, n.d.
oil on panel (AE, GIFT OF DRS. ALFRED AND ISABEL BADER, 1985)

Inmate Fabricated Jewelry/Curio Box, 1980s
decoupage on reclaimed pine, lined with velvet (CSC)

13

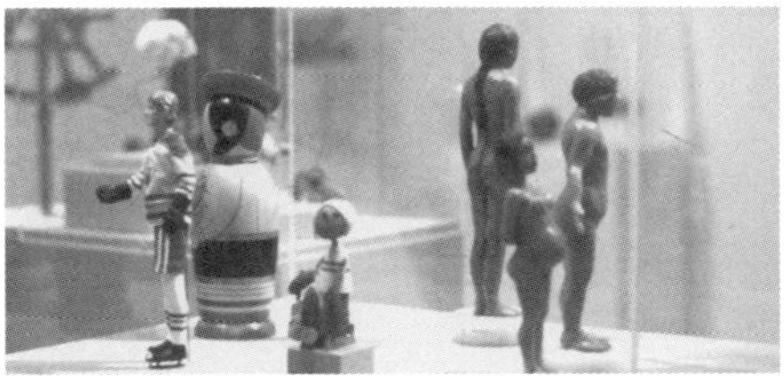

Wayne Gretzky Action Figure, c. 1981
plastic and polyester (IH)

Goalkeeper Doll (Romanian), c. 1975
wood, paint, copper, cotton, metal and paper (IH)

Matryoshka (Russian), c. 1975
painted wood (IH)

Marjorie Winslow
Wax Somatotypes, c. 1946
beeswax, talc, metal wire and oil paint
(MHC, ROBERTSON COLLECTION)

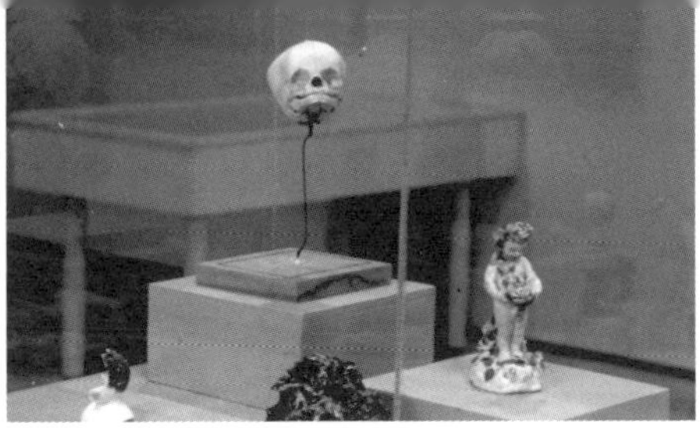

14

Excavated Doll's Head, c. 1900
porcelain (MT)

Human Infant Skull, early twentieth century
bone, metal and wood
(MHC, ROBERTSON COLLECTION)

"Baby's Hair" Silver (Cobalt, Ontario)
(MM, GIFT OF BILL AND ALAN AMOS IN MEMORY OF A.A. AMOS, 1997)

Child Figurine (European), n.d.
porcelain (AE)

15

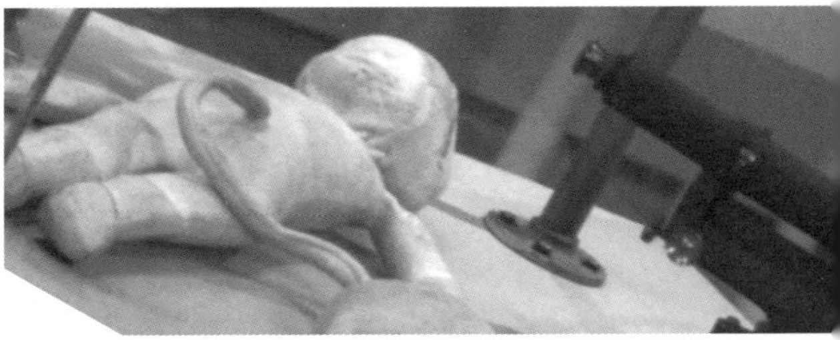

Instructional Model of Newborn,
early twentieth century
leather, rope and filler
(MHC, ROBERTSON COLLECTION)

Sextant, mid-twentieth century
brass and steel (MM)

Surveyor's Level, 1900s
(RMC, COURTESY RMC #57 LT. COL. H.S. GREENWOOD)

Theodolite (Japanese), 1940s
(RMC, COURTESY RMC #1971 BRIGADIER H.E. DeB. GREENWOOD)

16

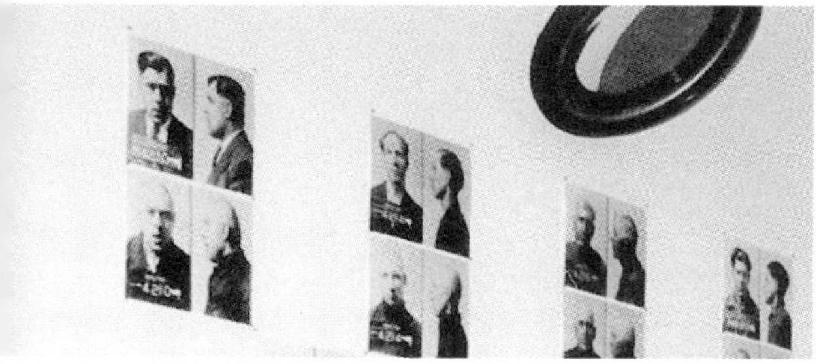

Concave Mirror, c. 1800
glass, wood, gesso and gilt frame (BH)

Kingston Penitentiary Admission Photographs, 1937
enlargements from 2 × 3" originals (CSC)

17

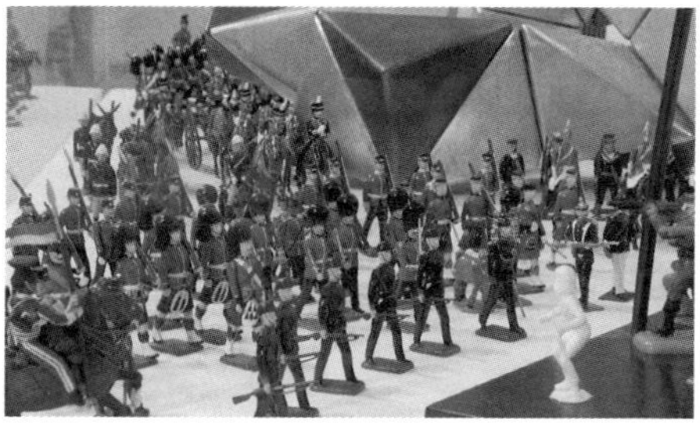

Robert Downing (Canadian, 1936–)
The Serpent, 1968
bronze and aluminum (AE, PURCHASED WITH THE ASSISTANCE OF ALUMNI CONTRIBUTIONS, 1973)

Hans Schleeh (Canadian, 1928–2001)
Family Tree, 1959
marble (AE, GIFT OF AYALA AND SAMUEL ZACKS, 1962)

Toy Soldiers, 1940s–2000
plastic and metal (RMC)

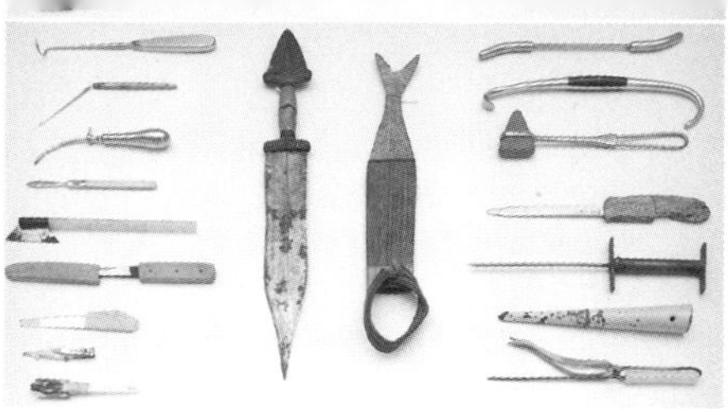

18

Surgical Instruments, nineteenth and twentieth centuries
mixed media, including stainless steel, nickel, chrome, rubber and plastic
(MHC)

Executioner's Knife (Ashanti), 1890s
metal and fish-skin (RMC, GIFT OF RMC #162 MAJOR-GENERAL SIR CASMIR VAN STRAUBENZEE)

Confiscated Inmate Shivs, 1950s–1980s
mixed media, including metal, glass, plastic, wood, tape, string, leather and paint (CSC)

19

Jacob Pynas (Dutch, c. 1585–1648)
The Stoning of St. Stephen, 1617
oil on panel (AE, GIFT OF DRS. ALFRED AND ISABEL BADER, 1983)

Diabase Dyke in Quartzite (Kingston, Ontario)
(MG)

Folded Rock (Sutton, Quebec)
(MG)

Tillite (Lake Huron, Ontario)
(MG)

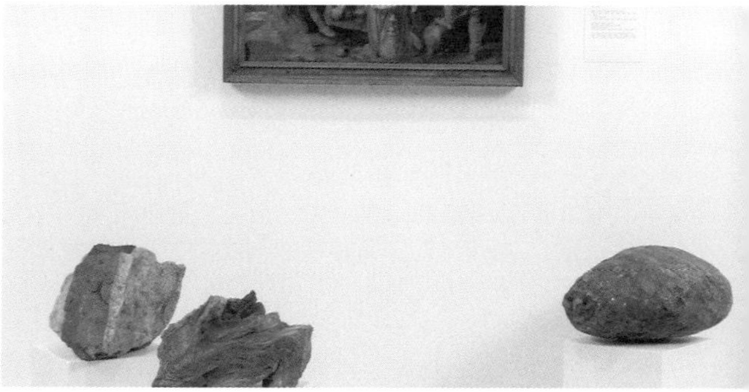

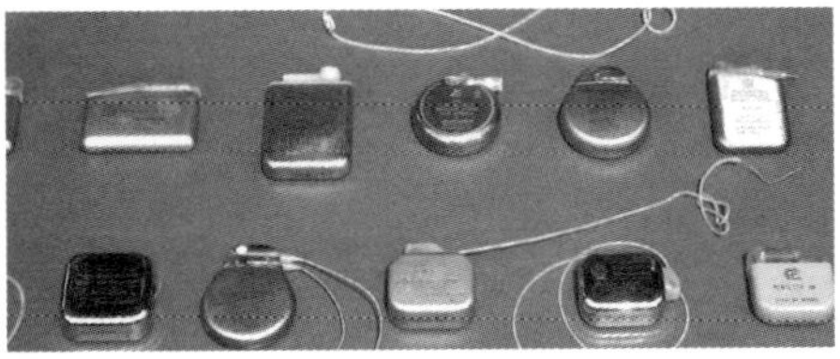

20

Pacemakers, 1960s–1990s
mixed media, including metal, plastic, rubber and electronics
(MHC, DONATION OF DR. WEST)

Life Rings, 1890s–1920s
styrofoam and hemp (MM)

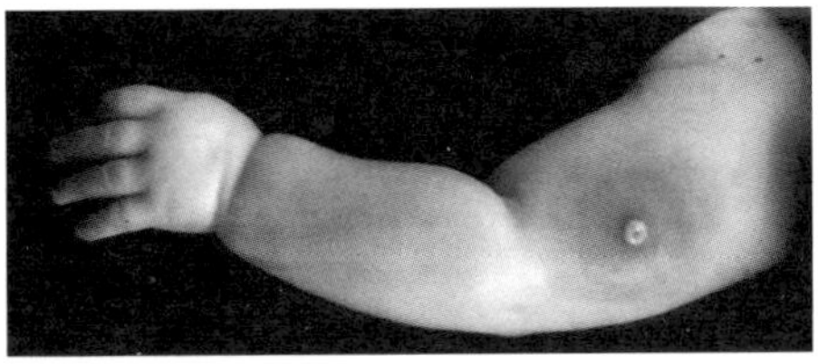

21

Joseph Towne
Baby's Arm Model with Vaccination Vesicle, 1890s
oil-painted wax, glass, metal and parchment
(MHC, FACULTY OF MEDICINE COLLECTION)

Fossilized Lizard in Amber
(MG)

Tobacco Case (Japanese), n.d.
wooden gall and wood (AE)

Douglas Arnberg
Views of Underwater Shipwrecks, 1999–2000
series of 10 digital prints

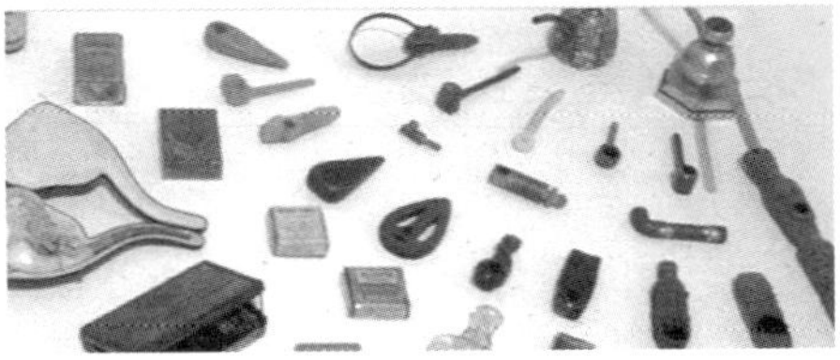

22

Confiscated Inmate Pipes, 1960s–1980s
mixed media, including wood, metal, paper and plastic (CSC)

Chocolate Tin Box (Australian), c. 1915
(RMC, PROPERTY OF RMC #25 SIR W.T. BRIDGES)

Patent Medicines, Packaged Herbs and Pharmaceuticals, nineteenth and twentieth centuries
mixed media, including metal, paper, plastic and glass (MHC, CHIONG AND PARKE-DAVIS COLLECTIONS)

Pipe (Austrian), c. 1875
meerschaum
(RMC, PRESENTED TO MR. HERBERT A. BAYNE)

23

Anthony Van Dyck, attributed to (Dutch, 1599–1641)
Ecce Homo, seventeenth century
oil on canvas (AE, GIFT OF DRS. ALFRED AND ISABEL BADER, 1986)

Poison Arrows (Papua New Guinea), n.d.
bamboo and wood (AE)

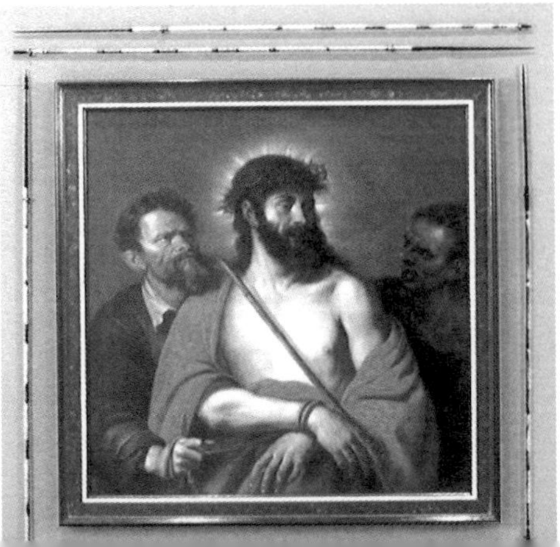

CATALOGUE OF ARTISTS' INTERVENTIONS

Diane Borsato
Mannequin Impossible, 2001
performance with slides, mannequin, cake

John Dickson
10 Small Nautical Disasters, 1996/97
including: Franklin Expedition, Leviathan, Oil Spill, Pearl Harbor, Sinking Ship, and *Titanic*
wine bottles, cork, water, and magnets
each 34 × 10 × 13 cm

John Dickson
Cyclone, 1997
bottle, sand, water, cork and copper ship, wooden cabinet, motor and electronic timer
55 × 55 × 135 cm

John Dickson
SOS, 2001
copper pipes, compressor, air bubbles, electronic timer and solenoid valves
270 × 100 cm

Fastwürms
Ms. Rockhound 2001, 2001
installation with photographs, painted banners, maps, yarn, crystals and rock samples

Jamelie Hassan
The Well, 2001
installation with objects from the museum's collection, the artist's personal archives, found and altered materials, ceramics, photography, drawings, watercolours, video

Peter Hobbs
Gothic, 2001
performance with live video

Barb Hunt
antipersonnel, 1998 – ongoing
knitted yarn, wood, lights
210 × 150 × 30 cm

Brian Jungen
Isolated Depiction of the Passage of Time, 2001
plastic trays, television monitor, VCR, western red cedar, light
112.5 × 117.5 × 100 cm

Vitaly Komar and Alexander Melamid with William McClelland
Call to Art, 2001
audio broadcast

Linda Montano
Forgiveness as Art, 2001
performance with Jessica Wyman

Anne Ramsden

Garden, 2001

installation with porcelain cups and saucers, seeds, text, artificial flowers and postcards

Clive Robertson

Speaking Tours, 2001

performance with Laurel Aziz, Jeff Brison, Jean Bruce, Lynda Jessup, Vojtech Jirat-Wasuitynski, Paul Kelley, Frances Leeming, Susan Lord, Jan Winton, and Jessica Wyman

Mitch Robertson

Famous™ Artstars, 1998

printed cards

5 × 7.5 cm

Mitch Robertson

World's Greatest, 2000

printed coffee mugs

dimensions variable

Mitch Robertson

Places I Have Been (Birth to Present), 2000 – ongoing

map with silver ink

130 × 85 cm

Mitch Robertson

Crowd Scene, 2001

video, 48 minutes, colour

Mitch Robertson

Lucky Numbers, 2001

21 keno cards, ink, brass

each 13 × 13 cm

Mitch Robertson

My Hall of Fame, 2001

fifteen felt banners

each 45 × 60 cm

Mitch Robertson

People I Know, 2001

five photographs with silver leaf

each 12.5 × 17.5 cm

Mitch Robertson

World's Largest Ball of Hockey Tape, 2001

approximately 36 km of hockey sock tape, dimensions increasing, tape donated by Renfrew Hockey Tape

Joyce Wieland

Sailboat, 1967

16 mm colour film transferred to videotape, 4 minutes

Mel Ziegler

Mail Order Authenticity, 2001

installation with furniture, utensils, household items

BIOGRAPHIES

DIANE BORSATO is an artist based in Montreal. Her projects include *Recognizing the Taste of Love*, which gave awards to select Montreal restaurants, and *The Self Love Project*, for Le Mois de la Performance at La Centrale. Most recently, in *HOW TO MAKE A SCULPTURE IN AN EMERGENCY* at Galerie Skol, the artist organized a successful sixty-person effort to build the world's longest paper clip chain according to Guinness World Records. Borsato earned degrees at York University (1997) and Concordia University (2001), and has published on her work in *The Drama Review*.

JOHN DICKSON completed his BFA at Queen's University (1986) and obtained his MFA from York University (1989). Based in Toronto, he is a founding member of the Nether Mind Toronto collective (1991–1995). He has exhibited throughout Canada and Europe, and has had solo exhibitions at the Koffler Gallery, Mercer Union, and the Robert Birch Gallery. In 1995, *Hermit IV — The Meridian Crossings* was presented at the Plasy Monastery, Czech Republic, and the following year he participated in *Container 96 Across Oceans*, in Copenhagen. He has received awards from the Toronto Arts Council, Ontario Arts Council, and the Canada Council.

JIM DROBNICK and **JENNIFER FISHER** are the founding members of DisplayCult, a collaborative framework for interdisciplinary studies in the visual arts. Based in Montreal, they write, curate, organize conferences, and produce art. Recent curatorial projects include *CounterPoses* and *Vital Signs*. They are currently editing anthologies on human exhibition, *Living Display* (University of Chicago Press), on the senses in art and culture, *Uncommon Senses*, and on sound practices, *Aural Cultures* (YYZ). Jennifer Fisher teaches at Concordia University, where she graduated from the Humanities Doctoral Program. Jim Drobnick teaches at Concordia University and is Assistant Editor at *Parachute* art magazine.

Formed in 1979 by Kim Kozzi and Dai Skuse, **FASTWÜRMS** is the trademark and joint authorship of these Toronto/Creemore-based artists. Fastwürms has exhibited and produced public commissions across Canada and in the United States, Europe and Japan. In 1997 they completed the installation of multiple sculptures *Turtled Pond*, *Snomun* and *Woodpecker Column* at the Metro Toronto Convention Centre. In 2000, *Ex Ovo Omnia* was permanently installed at the Macdonald Stewart Art Centre. Recent exhibitions include *Superstition* at Gallery TPW and *Rococo Tattoo* at the Power Plant.

JAMELIE HASSAN studied at the Academy of Fine Arts, Rome (1967), the École des Beaux Arts, Beirut (1968), the University of Windsor (1969) and the University of Mustansyria, Baghdad (1978–79). In 2001, she received the Governor General's Award in Visual Arts. Based in London, Ontario, she has had solo shows throughout Canada, including the National Gallery of Canada, and has exhibited widely internationally. Recent projects include *Trespassers & Captives* and *L'Espace d'Alphabet*. She was recently awarded artist-in-residence through the Canada Council for the Arts International Residency Program at the Contemporary Caribbean Arts in Port of Spain, Trinidad.

PETER HOBBS works in video, installation and performance. He has earned degrees at the Ontario College of Art (1988), the University of Toronto (1992), and Concordia University (2000). He has shown at Mercer Union, Gallery 101, the Montreal Telegraph Gallery, and the Nunnery Gallery in London, among other places. *Art-Throb*, a curatorial project examining the relationship between obsession and art, was exhibited at Galerie Articule. He is now pursuing a doctoral degree in Visual and Cultural Studies at the University of Rochester.

BARB HUNT obtained a Diploma in Visual Art from the University of Manitoba (1982) and an MFA from Concordia University (1994). She lives in Corner Brook, Newfoundland, and teaches sculpture and drawing at Sir Wilfred Grenfell College. She has exhibited in solo shows across Canada, including the Art Gallery of Ontario, Latitude 53, Plug-In Gallery, Artspace, Ace Art Inc. and the Kitchener/Waterloo Art Gallery. She has also participated in group shows such as *Meat* (107 Church St. and Galerie 418) and *A Dress: States of Being* (Art Gallery of North Dakota and Winnipeg Art Gallery).

BRIAN JUNGEN is a Vancouver-based artist of Swiss and Dunne-Za descent. He studied at Concordia University and in 1992 graduated from the Emily Carr Institute of Art and Design. He has been featured in solo shows at the Contemporary Art Gallery, Or Gallery, YYZ Artist's Outlet, the Dunlop Art Gallery and the Charles

H. Scott Gallery (who also published the catalogue *Brian Jungen*, 2000). Jungen is represented by the Catriona Jeffries Gallery and received a Viva Award from the Jack and Doris Shadbolt Foundation for the Visual Arts.

VITALY KOMAR and **ALEXANDER MELAMID** attended the Moscow Art School (1958–1960) and the Stroganov Institute of Art and Design (1962–1967). Collaborating since 1965, they are celebrated for the initiation of the SOTS art movement, the Soviet version of Conceptual and Pop Art. They immigrated to the US in 1978 and are currently based in New York. Their work is internationally acclaimed and represented in museum collections worldwide. Publications on their work include Carter Ratcliff, *Komar & Melamid*, JoAnn Wypijewski, *Painting by Numbers*, and Dave Eggars, *When Elephants Paint*. **WILLIAM McCLELLAND** studied at the University of Michigan and received a music degree from the Longy School of Music (1974). His compositions have been performed throughout the US and he has performed and produced recordings on the New World and Albany record labels. He has collaborated with Komar and Melamid on a number of projects since 1996.

LINDA MONTANO is a performance artist, the founder of The Art/Life Institute, Kingston, New York, and teacher of the form in numerous universities. Earning degrees at the Villa Schifanoia, Florence (1966), and the University of Wisconsin (1969), she has performed "living art" at museums, galleries and public sites worldwide. Her publications include *Art in Everyday Life*, *Performance Artists Talking in the Eighties*, and a forthcoming anthology of writings on her work. She has been featured at The New Museum (New York) and the Institute for Contemporary Art (London), and included in the exhibitions *Out of Actions* (LA MOCA) and *Endurance* (Exit Art). Her videos are distributed by Video Data Bank.

ANNE RAMSDEN received a BA from Queen's University (1973), a BFA from the Nova Scotia College of Art and Design (1977), and an MFA from Concordia University (1983). She teaches at the Université du Québec à Montréal, where she directs the Masters Program in Visual and Media Arts. Her work has been exhibited across Canada as well as in the United States, Japan and Europe. Recent shows include *Vancouver Perspective* (Taipei Fine Arts Museum) and *Anastylosis: Inventory* (Galerie d'art du Centre culturel de l'Université de Sherbrooke and Galerie UQÀM). Ramsden is represented by the Catriona Jeffries Gallery.

CLIVE ROBERTSON is an artist, independent curator and cultural critic teaching contemporary art history, arts policy studies and performance at Queen's University. Having earned degrees at Cardiff College of Art (1967) and the University of Reading (1971), he is completing a doctoral degree in Communication Studies at Concordia University. He has produced numerous performances, audio works, videotapes and installations since 1970. He is the co-author of *Performance au/in Canada*, 1970–1990, and the founding editor-publisher of *FUSE* magazine. Recent projects include *Talking Archive Toolshed* and *Speaking Volumes*.

Toronto-based **MITCH ROBERTSON** served three years in York University's BFA program before leaving for the Toronto School of Art where he graduated in 1997. His work has been shown in England, Australia, New Zealand, Northern Ireland, Switzerland, the United States and throughout Canada. Recent exhibitions include *Original Copy* (Gallery TPW), *Quoting Commercialism* (Walter Phillips Gallery), *In All the Wrong Places* (Ottawa Art Gallery), and *Stories for Grandchildren* (also published as an artist's book).

JOYCE WIELAND (1931–1998) lived in Toronto and New York, where she produced influential work in a diverse range of media. Major retrospective exhibitions were held at the National Gallery of Canada (1971) and the Art Gallery of Ontario (1987). In 1983, she was named an Officer of the Order of Canada. Her films have been screened internationally and are featured in *The Films of Joyce Wieland*, edited by Kathryn Elder, and Lauren Rabinovitz, *Points of Resistance*.

MEL ZIEGLER studied at the Rhode Island School of Design (1974–76), received a BFA from the Kansas City Art Institute (1978) and completed an MFA at the California Institute of Arts (1982). From 1978 to 1995 Ziegler collaborated with his late partner Kate Ericson, and has exhibited at the New Museum, the Whitney Museum of American Art, the Hirshhorn, and in shows such as *Places with a Past* (Charleston) and *Museum as Muse* (Museum of Modern Art). Based in Austin, he teaches sculpture at the University of Texas and maintains a studio in Milanville, PA.